# GO AND BE RECONCILED

# GO AND BE RECONCILED

## ALABAMA METHODISTS CONFRONT RACIAL INJUSTICE, 1954–1974

## WILLIAM E. NICHOLAS

### FOREWORD BY G. WARD HUBBS

NewSouth Books

Montgomery

NewSouth Books
105 S. Court Street
Montgomery, AL 36104

Library of Congress Cataloging-in-Publication Data is available on request.
Trade Paper: ISBN-13: 978-1-58838-325-9
Ebook: ISBN-13: 978-1-60306-415-6

Design by Randall Williams
Printed in the United States of America

*To G. Ward Hubbs*
*Mentor, Friend and Colleague*

# Contents

# Foreword

G. WARD HUBBS

In looking at the civil rights movement, we have become accustomed to the grand histories that focus on the leadership of a Martin Luther King Jr. or the simple courage of a Rosa Parks. And we have heard over and again about the decisive changes that followed dramatic events like Freedom Summer or such legislation as the 1964 Civil Rights Act. The effects of these people, laws, and protests are still being played out today. From the usual perspective, looking down from Mount Olympus, the events of the 1950s and '60s seem part of America's inexorable march from darkness to light. But when viewed from the ground up, we find another story: richer, more complex, and less certain.

Thus William Nicholas chose wisely in deciding to look at how Alabama Methodists, particularly those in north Alabama, weathered those times. Alabama was, of course, the site of many of the most important events of the civil rights movement—including the Freedom Riders, the Birmingham protests, the Sixteenth Street Baptist Church bombing, and the Selma to Montgomery march. Alabama Methodists were thus forced to face the racism in their midst more directly than nearly all other Americans.

Nicholas's look at these Methodists is also a look at what happens when individuals and local associations react to mandates issued from afar. The General Conference of the Methodist Church declared that its segregated structure would end, yet it was many years before the process to do so was implemented in Alabama. Through his extensive interviews with the participants, Nicholas reconstructs the delicate and sometimes tortuous path that desegregation took.

And his choice is particularly wise because as Christians, white Alabama

Methodists were forced to come to terms with the contradictions between the comfortable segregated world in which they lived and the Biblical teachings in which they believed. Nicholas shows these contradictions playing out in jails, newspapers, camps, and pulpits. Birmingham Public Safety Commissioner Eugene "Bull" Connor, for example, who was largely responsible for many of the worst attacks on black protesters, was known to challenge his minster at Woodlawn Methodist Church during sermons preaching against segregation. Others talked of secession from the Methodist Church.

It required walking a fine line to dismantle the church's segregated structure while keeping in the fold many who still favored segregation. The process required the arrival of a new bishop, Bishop Kenneth Goodson who—through personal persuasion and appointive prerogatives—was largely responsible for collapsing segregated Methodism in Alabama.

In the end, *Confronting Racial Injustice in the Deep South* tells us more than just how some Alabama Methodists made it through a turbulent era. It tells us something about patience, the importance of the right people in the right places, and of unflagging commitment.

*G. Ward Hubbs, professor emeritus of Birmingham-Southern College, is the archivist for the North Alabama Conference of the United Methodist Church and has published extensively on nineteenth-century Alabamians' thought and values.*

# Preface

During the climactic years of the civil rights movement, a closely related struggle was going on within the major Protestant denominations. This book looks carefully at how Alabama Methodists finally broke down their segregated church structure.

The process confounded expectations. During the 1950s and '60s the Methodist Church (which in 1967 would become the United Methodist Church) was slowly moving to disestablish its segregated structure under a mandate from its national governing body. Those outside the South generally assumed that, as in the past, national directives would simply be implemented locally, as they had in the past. They were mistaken. The Methodist Church, while hierarchical in structure, still reserved a great deal of influence to subordinate organizations, to local churches, and to strong lay members of those churches. Many Southern whites resisted what the General Conference, the Methodist Church's national governing body, had to say about race. Without a change in leadership on the state level, local resistance would prevail and the church's racially segregated structure would continue indefinitely. This situation was manifestly evident in Alabama where the two white Methodist conferences were committed to segregation at all levels of the institution's organization.

With notable exceptions, most historical studies of the civil rights movement look down from the top. Those studies may examine local events, for example freedom rides or the Selma to Montgomery march, but as episodes that led to national legislation or perhaps contributed to the careers of national political figures. Few historical studies look at the civil rights movement from the other direction, from how national issues played out on the local level. Fewer still have examined the critical role that individuals played in getting specific religious groups at the state level to deal with the challenge of overcoming racial division.

It was in this context that I decided to look closely at individuals in one limited region at the heart of the civil rights struggle: Alabama, especially north Alabama, from 1954 to 1974. There Martin Luther King Jr. stood up to Police Commissioner Eugene "Bull" Connor. But so did such unheralded individuals as a student studying for the ministry, Tommy Reeves, and Connor's own pastor at Woodlawn Methodist, John Rutland. I was intrigued by the inherent clash posed by an institution struggling to reconcile the moral teachings of Christ with the immorality of racism and legal segregation it faced within its own ranks.

Other works have already looked at either Alabama or the Methodist Church during the civil rights movement, and have done so with great effect.[1] I found, however, that too much involvement in the arguments for racial merger in the national church deflected attention from the very real issues at the local level; indeed, an account of the debates at the national level were really not the central theme of the story I wanted to tell. So this study is much more tightly focused. What sounds like an unnecessarily limiting decision, however, turned out instead to be an immensely broadening tactic as it helped me better to understanding how moral individuals decide to act in an immoral world.

The good fortune of my choice became ever clearer as my research progressed. I began with the holdings of the North Alabama Conference Archive at Birmingham-Southern College. These records, I quickly discovered, not only were heavily biased towards an institutional approach to my problem, but the official reports seemed to gloss over or even omit controversy—perhaps inadvertently, but I believe deliberately. My hopes at discovering anything remotely close to the actual workings of the process rested on interviewing the participants in the events over what the Methodist Church euphemistically called "merger," the dissolving of the black structures into the white. Several of those individuals, to my great regret, are now no longer living. And, quite frankly, I also regret that when I tried to talk to a few of the still-living important players in this episode, including a very prominent black participant, I was rebuffed. But to all of those who willingly talked to me about what for them were disturbing years, I owe a great debt. Their accounts were fascinating, went well beyond those vague and uninformative official documents, and provided essential inside information. More importantly, in moving their spoken words onto the printed page, I sensed that I was telling their long-suppressed stories for the first time. They spoke of a tumultuous time, the 1960s, when people of good will sometimes behaved heroically and sometimes behaved shamefully. I found their words compelling. These oral history interviews provided the core of my work. Without them, the official papers of the church available in the archives do not tell the complete story nor convey the intensity of the church's debate over desegregation.

After my debt to those involved, I wish to express a debt to others for generous help given me during my research of the last twelve years. Two stand out. The first is Guy Hubbs, curator of the North Alabama Conference Archive, who was able to guide me through the maze of boxes of newspapers, church histories and flyers, and the collection of the bishops' papers and letters. The second was an outstanding undergraduate student at Birmingham-Southern, Mitch Robinson, who spent the spring of 2000 working on an oral history project in which he talked to many of the same people that I did; those conversations were preserved on cassette tapes in the archives for general use. Both Mitch and I had to be acutely aware of the limitations of memory when considering events of the past, but I have tried to corroborate our interviewees' memories with others' and to check them against printed sources. In the end, of course, there are contradictions and varying assessments of the importance of certain persons and events within the narratives. The story of the integration of the North Alabama Conference is not a simple one, and the complexity of viewpoints is what for me makes social history such a challenging but at the same time revealing field of historical research.

I would also be remiss if I did not acknowledge the support of Birmingham-Southern College in granting me two sabbatical leaves to work on this project, and the encouragement and advice given to me by my very helpful colleagues in the History Department: Mark Lester, Victoria Ott, Randall Law, and Matt Levey. Without this support I would not have been able to find the time to complete the study. Finally, I acknowledge the constant love and longtime support of my late wife, Mary Ellen Nicholas, who gave me her unstinting criticism of my written prose and encouraged me to pursue this research in the midst of a busy teaching schedule.

## NOTES

1.  See, for example Donald E. Collins, *When the Church Bell Rang Racist: The Methodist Church and The Civil Rights Movement in Alabama* (Macon, Georgia, Mercer University Press, 1998); and in a different context, J. Mills Thornton III, *Dividing Lines: Municipal Politics and the Struggle for Civil Rights in Montgomery, Birmingham, and Selma* (Tuscaloosa: University of Alabama Press, 2002).

# GO AND BE RECONCILED

# Introduction

# Methodists and Race

The 1954 Supreme Court decision outlawing segregated schools, *Brown v. Board of Education,* caused a variety of reactions from white Southerners. Longtime segregationists, including many political leaders, responded to the judicial challenge defensively and sometimes aggressively—both individually and through their institutions. Within the mainline Protestant denominations of the South, the *Brown* decision came at a time when the Methodist Church nationally was rethinking its policies on race and race relations. Race was not a new issue to the Methodists: the denomination had acknowledged and debated the contradictions in racial separation since the early nineteenth century. But the school desegregation decision forced Methodists to confront the matter without equivocation.

The direction they took shared the Court's thinking in one overarching assumption: those Methodists who pushed for the church to desegregate, like those who resisted, believed that preserving racial distinctions depended on preserving segregated institutions. To put it another way, all Methodists believed—mistakenly it would turn out—that changes in attitudes would follow from changes in structures. Because the Methodist Church was organized hierarchically rather than by congregation, the crucial civil rights battles would thus be waged over whether to preserve or to destroy the racially distinct organizations within church structure, particularly the annual conferences—more so than within the individual churches. Alabama in 1954 was typical. The Methodist churches in the state were organized into three Annual Conferences (so named because they met once a year): the all-white Alabama-West Florida Conference and North Alabama Conference, and the all-black Central Alabama Conference.

For nearly two centuries American Methodists had already faced the contradictions in racial separation with a dynamic yet complex organizational structure. John Wesley, the brilliant Anglican priest, began the Methodist movement by preaching—in open fields and other unorthodox places—to those displaced by England's emerging Industrial Revolution. "The world is my parish," he famously declared. Wesley's message rested largely on giving hope to those who had none. He declared that "God willeth all men to be saved," explicitly denying the orthodox Calvinist position that only a few are selected for salvation and the rest are eternally damned. Wesley's message fell on receptive ears, especially to those ordinary people overlooked by a complacent and self-satisfied Anglican Church.

But it was in America that Methodism took hold, beginning in Baltimore in 1784 with the founding of the Methodist Episcopal Church (MEC). The new denomination resonated with Americans. Wesley stressed that all could be saved because—in the words of the Declaration of Independence—all had been created equal, at least in God's eyes. Methodists were thus optimistic, as were Americans. Methodists believed that the common man could be reformed, that we could do better. Americans believed the same thing, for the country would soon be entering an age of reform with the Second Great Awakening, creating institutions for education and social betterment. Methodists would be at the forefront of these efforts.

Methodists not only had the right theology for America, they had the right organization. Future Bishop Francis Asbury, appointed by Wesley in 1784 as a superintendent in America, established an itinerant ministry of young preachers on horseback. Known as circuit riders, they would be crucial to Methodism's success in spreading the message to those living on the frontier. But circuit riders were not entirely on their own. They were backed by what eventually became a large and complicated organization.

At the top was the General Conference, the governing body of clergy and laity that met every four years to decide and revise the denomination's policy and doctrine. The General Conference body had "full legislative powers over all matters" that were "connectional"—in other words, just about everything beyond the daily operations of the individual churches.[1] The General Conference defined church membership, established qualifications for its ministers, and ultimately arranged the election of bishops to head the Annual Conferences. An equal number of clerical and lay delegates were elected proportionally by each conference to attend the quadrennial meetings of the General Conference.

The policies established at the General Conferences were then expected to be executed by the Annual Conferences that exercised administrative authority over geographical regions, usually a state or part of a state. As the denomination's official statement of doctrine, the *Discipline*, put it, the "annual conference is the basic body in the church." (For certain functions Annual Conferences were grouped into ultimately five regionally defined white jurisdictions and one black jurisdiction that covered the entire country.) It was at the Annual Conference level that the struggle to end racial distinctions would concentrate. Conferences were in turn divided into districts made up of individual churches. Outside this established hierarchical system, the Methodists created a dizzying number of *ad hoc* organizations on national and local levels, comprising both laity and clergy, to deal with such topics as temperance and education.

Presiding over the Annual Conferences were bishops. They wielded considerable power that included ordaining, admitting, and assigning ministers to their local churches. Under the bishop were the district superintendents, ordained ministers who served as liaisons between the bishop and the ministers and coordinated the efforts of the individual churches within their districts. Thus the district superintendents both advised the bishop and carried out the bishop's policies. As a student of Methodist Church district organization explained, the district superintendent is "the connector, the visible symbol to the laity of the local church" of Methodism as a whole.[2] Not uncommonly, district superintendents in Alabama were often caught between the viewpoints of local Methodist congregations and the official mandates of the national church; their inclination was to avoid confrontation over the denomination's controversial policies as much as possible. But the intent of the structure was clear. Church pastors, appointed by the bishop in consultation with the district superintendents, were expected to comply with and implement mandates emanating from the General Conference.[3]

The laity's part in church policy was somewhat limited. Methodist lay members were represented in the power structure by electing one representative to the annual conference from each pastoral charge or church appointment. Although their numbers were equivalent to those of the ministers, their power was not proportional in all matters. These laity could not vote, for example, on "matters of ordination, character, and conference relations of ministers."[4] That being said, the local racial environment in the South would strongly influence the attitude of Methodist laity toward any change in the denomination's racial structure. In practice, any pastor who wanted to stay in his pulpit for the usual four-year appointment would be hesitant not to reflect his congregation's viewpoints.

While the structure might seem rigid, especially to those from denominations comprised of the voluntary association of autonomous congregations (such as the Baptists), Methodism's often perplexing system of organizations was flexible and vigorous. When combined with its message of hope for all, Methodism grew to become the largest Protestant movement in nineteenth-century America.

Methodism would not remain monolithic, however, and from early on its most significant divisions centered on race. In 1794, only ten years after the denomination's founding, black Methodists in Philadelphia, Pennsylvania, began worshipping separately. In 1816, the African Methodist Episcopal Church (AME) was formally established in Philadelphia by black Methodists. Five years later, a half-dozen black congregations in New York created the African Methodist Episcopal Zion Church (AMEZ). These two denominations would confine their work to the North until the end of the Civil War.

During the 1840s even the Methodist Episcopal Church split over the issue of slavery. John Wesley had declared slave-holding to be inconsistent "with any degree of natural justice, mercy, and truth. . . . Liberty is the right of every human creature." The first American Methodists agreed and outlawed slavery in their 1784 convention. But Eli Whitney's cotton gin and the opening of vast lands in the Old Southwest changed all that. While slave ownership among Southern Methodists became common, some Northern abolitionists withdrew from the MEC and in 1843 formed the Wesleyan Methodist Church. The more serious division was precipitated the next year after James Osgood Andrew, a Methodist bishop in Georgia, married a woman who owned slaves. When the 1844 General Convention of the

MEC suspended Andrew, the Southern bishops withdrew and in 1845 created the Methodist Episcopal Church, South (MECS). Clergy and laity in the MECS defended slavery not only on political but on scriptural grounds. During the Civil War the MEC attempted to make inroads among freedmen and women, and the two denominations battled over church properties. U.S. Secretary of War Edwin Stanton (a Methodist) presented all MECS churches in occupied areas to the MEC, and Northern Methodist bishops even appointed agents to facilitate the transfer.[5]

After the war, the Methodist Episcopal Church (which white Southerners derisively labeled the "Northern Methodist Church") carried on intense missionary efforts in the South among white Unionists and freed African Americans. These MEC missionaries established biracial conferences; but due in part to white Southerners' resistance to worshipping with blacks and in part due to black Methodists' desires for self-government, beginning in 1876 the General Conference allowed racially separate conferences. Thus Alabama soon had two MEC conferences: the all-white Alabama Conference and the all-black Central Alabama Conference. By 1939, the nation's nineteen separate all-black annual conferences comprised about 315,000 members.[6]

Meanwhile, the other Methodist denominations were active among the freed people. The Methodist Episcopal Church, South had always encouraged black members, in part to keep tighter control over potential insurrectionists. But after Emancipation, black Methodists began fleeing the church of the former slaveholding establishment and its attendant theology of racial inferiority and dependency. As a consequence, in 1870 the MECS created an entirely separate church for its black membership: the Colored [now Christian] Methodist Episcopal Church (CME). The ties between the MECS and the CME remained close over the next half century as the white denomination extended financial support on a regular basis to the newer black denomination. Other segments of the black population in the South were attracted to the AME and the AMEZ; both all-black denominations had carried on missionary activities among Southern blacks following the Civil War. Essentially then, black Methodists in the South were presented with three alternatives to affiliation with the national Methodist Church: the

CME, the AME, and the AMEZ. These three offered autonomy in church structure and freedom from white influence or direction—in contrast to the MEC's segregated and subordinate conferences.[7]

A new spirit of reconciliation between the two white Methodist denominations emerged at the end of the nineteenth century. For a younger generation of church leaders, the sectional debates of the 1840s were long in the past, and the new Methodist leadership mirrored the political environment of racial relations nationwide. As the humanitarian efforts of the Republican Party on behalf of freedmen dwindled after Reconstruction, both national political parties shifted emphasis towards programs supporting business interests. Given "New South" promoters of industrialization and investment opportunities, combined with a federal government disinclined to interfere, the Democratic Party in the South moved rapidly toward legalized racial separation. The most important spokesman for Southern blacks, Booker T. Washington, delivered a message of accommodation to white businessmen in his "Atlanta Compromise" address of 1895. Whites also applied Darwin's evolutionary theories to society to justify a hierarchy based on race, and this in turn was used to justify the nation's new enthusiasm for world power and colonial possessions. The Methodist Episcopal Church found the new philosophy compatible with the establishment of mission fields in Africa and Asia. But the new missionary spirit did not apply to its black members in the South, who found their rights of citizenship now abridged in terms of political participation, educational opportunity, and legal restrictions on the races mixing in commercial and social settings.

By the 1930s, white Methodists in both North and South were negotiating to resolve the differences that had kept them apart since the 1840s. One issue dominated the discussions over a possible plan of union: what to do about the nineteen black conferences in the Methodist Episcopal Church. The commissioners on unification from the Methodist Episcopal Church, South would have preferred merger of these conferences into the all-black CME.[8] This proposal was unacceptable to both the black membership and the white leadership of the MEC.

At the critical 1939 Uniting Conference, white leaders of the two wings of Methodism compromised, over the objections of black members. They combined the MEC's all-black conferences into a single separate entity, the Central Jurisdiction, spanning the entire country. This new body was intended to be coequal with the five all-white jurisdictions, which were organized by region. The Central Jurisdiction could elect its own bishops and meet nationally every four years, have representatives on national church agencies and boards, publish its own materials, and organize youth and women's groups equivalent to their white counterparts. Although black congregations had rejected the plan when it was originally presented in 1936, most white Southern churches and their Northern counterparts voted overwhelmingly for it.

The main task of the delegates to the Uniting Conference, however, was to merge the Methodist Episcopal Church and the Methodist Episcopal Church, South (along with the much smaller Methodist Protestant Church) into a single denomination: the Methodist Church (which in 1968 would become the United Methodist Church). As for the segregated Central Jurisdiction, the new church structure was put into operation in 1940 at the first General Conference.[9] The white leadership had applied the prevailing political and constitutional ethos of that period: "separate but equal." There is no question that black congregations within the former MEC had been forced to accept a plan that they bitterly opposed. In the words of a young black clerical delegate to the 1940 General Conference, the new structure violated "the principle of brotherhood dominant in the life and teachings of Jesus."[10]

Although the leadership of the church might view their denomination as having resolved the sectional decisions that still marked their Baptist and Presbyterian counterparts, they had in fact created a structure compatible with segregationist ideology.[11] For the next decade and a half, the Methodist Church, at least in the South, would be reorganized as an integral part of a unified church in which whites were numerically superior. At the 1939 Uniting Conference, the Alabama Conference of the MEC had reported only 11,684 black members in the entire state of Alabama, whereas the two all-white MECS Alabama conferences—the North Alabama and the Alabama-West Florida (comprising the southern half of Alabama and much of the Florida panhandle)—reported 151,070 and 95,000 members respectively.[12] The majority of ministers and nearly all the laity in the North Alabama Conference did not question the separation of the denomination in Alabama into two racial groupings. In fact, they condoned the system and defended it, for this had been the major condition for their reunification with the national church.

An examination of the attitudes of the two white conferences toward racial relations reveals considerable uniformity on this and most social issues in the 1940s and early 1950s. Alabama Methodism during these years was experiencing dynamic growth in terms of local church facilities. Almost every week, the voice of the Methodist Church in Alabama, the *Alabama Christian Advocate,* reported the opening of a new sanctuary, fellowship hall, or church education building somewhere in the state. America's middle classes expanded in the 1950s as a result of the postwar population boom, and there was a corresponding growth in the membership of the mainline Protestant denominations.[13] By 1956 the North Alabama Conference (NAC) built a hospital and, in conjunction with the Alabama-West Florida Conference (A-WFC), supported a children's home and a home for the aging. On social reform, the *Advocate* devoted extraordinary attention to the evils of drink, a position that the Methodists had made their most important social doctrine in the nineteenth century. The editor of the *Advocate* in the 1940s even ascribed the success of Japan's attack on American forces at Pearl Harbor to the "drunkenness of our troops there."[14] And in 1951, the Alabama-West Florida Conference approved a resolution in which they moved to delete the word "wine" from the communion ritual of the Methodist Church and substitute for it "the cup" or "the fruit of the vine."[15] Temperance was a practice that most ministers enthusiastically endorsed in their weekly sermons; to some extent it represented what remained of Southern Progressivism.

On the issue of race relations, however, the *Advocate* was mostly silent. By far the most attention was given to the annual Race Relations Sunday each February for the support of Paine College in Augusta, Georgia. This Colored Methodist Episcopal college had started as a cooperative effort by the MECS and the CME to provide an education for African Americans. Paine traditionally had a white president and a black dean. The trustees and teaching faculty represented both races. Often white Methodist churches marked Race Relations Sunday by inviting a black gospel choir to perform or CME ministers to preach. Pastors told their congregations to remember that Paine College was a major home mission of the North Alabama Conference. In editorials preceding these Sundays, the *Advocate* would express a viewpoint on racial matters that probably reflected the outlook of most white Southerners on the issue. In a 1951 article, for example, a Georgia minister wrote that "customs, habit, traditions are strong in the mores of our people and we cannot force radical changes in race relations."[16] Few African American writers were invited to contribute to the *Advocate*, but one black student at Paine College did write an article that same year in which he testified to the "just and human qualities" of his white professors at Paine and the positive effect these persons had on his own view of white Southerners.[17] The *Advocate* entitled the article "Removing the Poison of Race Hatred." The editors of the newspaper generally seemed to be more interested in the numerous Methodist mission schools that the Methodists maintained in Africa than they were in the situation of African American churches within the Alabama Central Conference.

The *Advocate* was only reflecting the attitudes of its white readers. David Vann, a prominent young Methodist lawyer who early on attacked segregation in Birmingham, recalled that the prevailing mentality was to preserve the racial status quo. Many whites thought that segregation was wrong, but they "figured it wouldn't get changed until the people who had the economic ball decided that was a good thing to do."[18] Even though much of the Birmingham economy was controlled from the outside (U.S. Steel's extensive holdings, for example), Vann thought these business interests "didn't want to upset the local people" by challenging the separation of the races. A recent study of Birmingham's religious leadership has shown that as late as the early 1960s white Southern clergy were reluctant to take a public stand on racial issues because they thought that if change were to come, it must be through a process of "gradual accommodation of the South to new ways of thought and behavior."[19] This is not to say that some Methodist clergy and laity found segregation and scripture to be easily reconciled. But confrontation simply didn't seem to be how Southerners solved problems, and most white Methodists and their Protestant denominational counterparts preferred not to discuss racial issues in polite conversation.

Such was Methodism in Alabama as the civil rights movement began to unfold in response to the *Brown* decision of 1954.

## NOTES

1.   *Discipline of the Methodist Church* (Methodist Publishing House, 1956), 9–10.

2.   Jack Tuell. *The Organization of the United Methodist Church.* (Nashville: Abingdon Press, 1982), 105.

3.   The Methodist structure, partly originating in the Anglican model, shared similarities with the Roman Catholic Church hierarchy. The Catholic Church, too, had a top-down hierarchy with little local autonomy. Local Methodist and Catholic churches were not empowered to fire clergy.

4.   Ibid., 17.

5.   Charles Martin Prestwood, "Social Ideas of Methodist Ministers in Alabama since Unification," (Ph.D. Diss., Boston University, 1970), 80.

6.   J. Philip Wogaman, *Methodism's Challenge in Race Relations: A Study of Strategy* (Boston: Boston University Press, 1960), 1.

7.   Othal Hawthorne Lakey, *The History of the CME*, rev. ed. (Memphis: CME Publishing House, 1996), 113.

8.   Wogaman, *Methodism's Challenge*, 2.

9.   The entire denomination held a quadrennial meeting in which the bishops and representatives of the clergy and laity determined church policies and committee agendas for the next four years.

10.   James S. Thomas, *Methodism's Racial Dilemma* (Nashville: Abingdon Press,1992), 43.

11.   The Presbyterians would not unite until 1985, and the Baptists are still nationally divided; see chapter 5.

12.   *Journal of the North Alabama Conference of the Methodist Church* (1939), 179, 327.

13.   The *Alabama Christian Advocate* occasionally varied its title during its existence from its start in 1881 to its closure in 1994. For clarity and consistency, it will always be cited as the *Alabama Christian Advocate*.

14.   Prestwood, "Social Ideas," 181.

15.   Ibid., 174.

16.   *Alabama Christian Advocate*, February 11, 1951.

17.   Ibid. For the history of Paine College, see Mark K. Bauman, *Warren Akin Candler: The Conservative as Idealist* (Metuchen, NJ: Scarecrow Press, 1981).

18.   David Vann interview tape (n.d.) given by Ruth Vann Lillian to Mitch Robinson. North Alabama Conference Archives (hereinafter NACA), Birmingham-Southern College.

19.   Jonathan S. Bass, *Blessed Are the Peacemakers: Martin Luther King, Eight White Religious Leaders and the "Letter from Birmingham Jail"* (Baton Rouge: Louisiana State University Press, 2001), 4.

# I.

# The Debate over Desegregation and Race, 1954–1960

Two years after the *Brown* decision, Joe Elmore, a young Methodist Vanderbilt seminary graduate, entered the ministry in the North Alabama Conference. Elmore later recalled his impression that the church members of his day "misread the Bible in a gross kind of way." During his early ministry, Elmore found that his congregations did not understand the theological concept of grace as embodying an "unconditional love of God" that was "inclusive." Methodists were quite willing to accept the notion of "personal salvation" as a part of God's plan, but they would "resist to the death" the larger implication that "everybody is going to be *in*." Elmore believed that the issue came down to a fear of "losing members" and consequently undermining the church by "losing dollars."[1]

Other young NAC clergy such as Bill Davis thought that theology became secondary to the clergy's need to maintain their position in society. The topic of race or a discussion of it from the pulpit was a "kind of matter you had to play," he thought, "especially if you were ambitious politically, you couldn't alienate the majority." The members of the laity were more direct in their views. "If your preacher doesn't preach segregation from his pulpit," one recommended, "you cut his salary to a dollar a year and sell his parsonage."[2] Such threats implied that local congregations might dictate the denomination's position on racial relations, but such a viewpoint was contrary to the established structure of the Methodist Church. Indeed, resistance by Southern white Methodists to General Conference directives on civil rights would mark a new turn. The creation of the black denominations; the 1830s protest against episcopal power, which resulted in the formation of the Methodist Protestant Church; the 1840s secession of the

Southern churches and the subsequent creation of the Methodist Episcopal Church, South—all had been led by the clergy. This time the protest would come from the bottom up, for it was the laity that would resist the General Conference's directives on racial unification.

Despite a broad unwillingness to discuss race openly during the 1940s and early 1950s, a few Methodist white clergy and staff not only did so but even dared to challenge the status quo. Perhaps the earliest was Andrew S. Turnipseed, pastor of the Greenville First Methodist Church in south Alabama. A 1933 Birmingham-Southern College graduate who never attended seminary, the Reverend Turnipseed enjoyed a successful career as a result of his exceptional preaching ability. In the 1940s, he and other ministers and teachers helped to organize a state chapter of the Methodist Federation for Social Action (MFSA), a national organization that dated from the first decade of the twentieth century. Remaining small and unofficial, with Turnipseed as its leader, the Alabama MFSA provided a forum for the development of Methodist positions on social and economic issues.[3] By 1947 the chapter had about seventy members, thirty-two of whom were ministers. The social stances of the organization were not popular in Alabama (except, of course, for the usual emphasis on temperance). The Alabama chapter went on record in its *Bulletin* as endorsing "the brotherhood of man," a kind of code expression for attacking the denomination's current racial structure.[4] By 1950 the MFSA began to receive attention within Methodist ranks as an organization that supported racial equality and other radical causes—allegedly with some connection to communist ideology.

Probably no issue was more disruptive on the national political scene in the early 1950s than the American reaction to Soviet communism, and the MFSA helped draw the Methodist Church into this domestic conflict. This shift was reflected in a February 1950 *Reader's Digest* article, "Methodism's Pink Fringe." Written by Stanley High, a Presbyterian layman and graduate of Boston University School of Theology (a Methodist school), the essay portrayed the MFSA as providing a platform for Soviet Union apologists.[5] The resulting publicity divided national Methodist leadership. Some prominent Methodist resigned their membership in the organization, while others rushed to its defense by arguing that the MFSA was being subjected to a smear campaign.[6] Although doctrinaire leftists undoubtedly belonged to the organization, the majority of its five thousand members supported the official Methodist Church position of strong opposition to communism.

Turnipseed and his colleagues found themselves under a concerted attack. The tensions of the Cold War and the resulting McCarthyism had given Methodist conservatives a new and convenient strategy for attacking non-conformist social ideas. In January 1950, a group of laymen in the Bessemer District (west of Birmingham) had a meeting in Central Park Methodist Church in which the district superintendent, G. M. ("Mont") Davenport, reported on the *Reader's Digest* article and labeled the MFSA not merely pink but "actually red in its leadings toward Russian Communism." The intent of the meeting was to condemn the MFSA and to demand that the NAC withdraw support from or break any ties with the group. The *Alabama Christian Advocate*'s conservative editor, Joshua Arthur Gann Jr., joined the fray by printing a piece in February asserting that the MFSA was "a seedbed of Communism, employing the techniques of the demagogue as it appeals to class bitterness and stirs racial antagonism."[7] The author of this essay, G. Stanley Frazer, was soon to emerge as a ministerial spokesman for the segregationist front among Methodists in Montgomery. The desired response to these allegations came at the annual meeting of the North Alabama Conference in October 1950 when the assembled delegates adopted a resolution that condemned communism and severed "any connection" with the MFSA.[8] Superintendent Davenport attached an amendment that committed the conference to "segregation in church and society" and supported continuation of the all-black Central Jurisdiction. By inference, then, the resolution equated communism with any move by the denomination to desegregate. The Reverend Turnipseed and his cohorts decided at the end of 1950 to allow the MFSA to die as they were unable to defend and sustain its program within the prevailing social environment of Alabama Methodism. Turnipseed himself turned to involvement in civil rights efforts in south Alabama, particularly in the Mobile area, an activity that was later to be problematic for the Alabama-West Florida Conference.

Two ministers in the North Alabama Conference, Daniel C. Whitsett and John Rutland provided the other important liberal voices of Turnipseed's generation in the 1950s. Whitsett, who was at Sylacauga First Methodist Church from 1947 to 1958, was the NAC equivalent to Turnipseed. Sylacauga was located in a northeastern part of the state where the Ku Klux Klan was active, and Whitsett and his wife Julia constantly drew hostile attention from the KKK because of their outspokenness on racial issues. Whitsett's sermons were often devoted to racial justice topics, and he was forceful in his vision of a society in which racial barriers would not exist.[9] Whitsett brought many non-Alabamians and even black ministers from the Central Alabama Conference to preach in his pulpit in Sylacauga.[10] The KKK burned crosses on the lawn of his parsonage in retaliation. His continued advocacy of integration influenced a number of young Methodists who were bound for seminary but made it almost impossible to move him to another church in Alabama. Whitsett spent an almost unprecedented eleven years in Sylacauga before a new bishop, Bachman G. Hodge, managed with the help of Whitsett's friends to secure him an appointment in 1958 to a church in Cambridge, Massachusetts, near Harvard University. Paul Hardin Jr., then pastor of Birmingham First Methodist Church, had explained in a letter to Hodge that Whitsett would not "lift a finger to arrange a move outside this Conference," but that he had agreed to leave Sylacauga if the bishop found him another post.[11] Whitsett went into exile in the northeast, and Bill Davis among others thought that the "real symbol of progress" had left the North Alabama Conference.[12]

Whitsett's fellow NAC racial moderate, the Reverend John Rutland, was assigned from 1953 to 1962 to Woodlawn Methodist Church in a middle-class suburb in the eastern part of Birmingham. He had begun his long career as a Methodist preacher in 1933. By the time he arrived at Woodlawn, he had already aroused the wrath of the Tuscaloosa Klan for having invited a black gospel quartet to perform before a racially mixed audience in his church there. At Woodlawn, in a part of the city where "white flight" to the suburbs was in progress, he preached against segregation. On occasion, Rutland even invited a black minister to deliver a sermon. Woodlawn's church bulletin often included Rutland's thoughts on racial inclusiveness taken directly from his sermons. Among the members of his congregation was Birmingham's public safety commissioner, Eugene

("Bull") Connor, who denounced Rutland for his "nigger-preaching." On more than one Sunday, the police superintendent would stand up in the pew and interrupt Rutland's sermon to disagree, Rutland recalled in his autobiography.[13] His wife, Mary, endured periodic threatening calls from the Klan, and once while the Rutlands were away on a trip a cross was burned in the yard of the parsonage.[14] Despite all this adversity, Rutland, who was small in stature but big in bravery, received the steadfast support of many of his Woodlawn members. As the chair of his stewardship board put it, "Brother John Rutland has the courage to say what we need to hear, even if at times we do not want to hear the truth he speaks."[15]

From his bishop and many of his fellow clergy, however, the Reverend Rutland received so little support that he described his tenure at Woodlawn as years of "loneliness and fear . . . sometimes we felt abandoned and forsaken." Bishop Hodge was particularly concerned about Rutland's continuing to preach on what he called "the race question," and more than once the bishop tried to arrange to transfer him out of Alabama. Although Rutland was allowed to remain at Woodlawn, Hodge never praised him for his courage and in fact admonished him to stop printing sermon excerpts in his weekly church bulletin where segregationists might encounter his ideas in print. In the end, the bishop admitted to Rutland, "I want you to move . . . but where could I put you?"[16]

Bishop Hodge's view of Rutland was not shared by all the clergy, however, and those bulletins so disliked by Hodge motivated some younger clergy. Joe Elmore remembered saving Woodlawn Church bulletins as an inspiration.[17] According to Elmore, the Reverend Rutland gave "strong witness" to young pastors like himself, and he recalled going with him to see a movie at a black Congregational church on Center Street where it was illegal under segregation laws for whites to be seated. While some Methodist ministers regarded Rutland as a gadfly on the racial front, Elmore thought that no one else "stood so firmly in the face of bishops and others." That the establishment called Rutland a "troublemaker" seemed to make him even feistier.[18]

While Rutland and Whitsett seem to have been the most important advocates for racial justice among the North Alabama Conference clergy in the early 1950s, a layperson was quietly desegregating gatherings at Camp

Sumatanga, the NAC's sprawling camp in the hills northeast of Birmingham. This was Nina H. Reeves, a remarkable young woman who would work for the conference until 1996. A Mississippian from Yazoo City, Reeves had attended Millsaps College and taken a part-time job with the Wesley Foundation while doing graduate work at the University of Alabama.[19] She became the NAC youth director in 1947 and four years later began to work at the recently opened Camp Sumatanga, conducting numerous summer programs designed for young people. She had grown up in a family grocery business that served many black customers, and she early on decided that the separation of blacks into the Central Jurisdiction was "ridiculous" and "silly." As youth director, Reeves began quietly to integrate the summer activities at the camp. In the summer of 1955, she invited Dr. Julius S. Scott Jr., future president of Paine College and a close friend, to speak to one of the senior youth gatherings. Reeves admired Scott, recalling later that she wasn't "thinking about black and white; this was my friend Julius Scott who was a tremendous preacher and probably was more intelligent than those guys who were saying he couldn't come." Reeves knew that she would have to "operate" within the system, and she persuaded the conference's Board of Christian Education to allow Scott to come if he stayed in the infirmary away from everybody else and sat at a separate table to eat his meals in the dining hall. Scott not only spent the entire week with the students, but from his second meal on "there were so many people sitting at his table, there was no place for him to sit." When the Sumatanga trustees discovered what had happened, there were threats to fire Reeves; but her friends on the conference Board of Christian Education were able to protect her job by assuring the trustees that it would never happen again. Later, Reeves would explain her courageous support of Scott's appearance as simply "the right thing to do." The trustees were so shaken by the episode that they fired all the camp's black cooks as retribution. Reeves continued her advocacy of interracial contacts behind the scenes, and her "citizenship tours" in the 1950s with teenagers to visit Washington, D.C., and the United Nations soon earned her the label of a "communist" who was corrupting Methodist youth. She was no doubt influential with young people. A Methodist Youth Fellowship participant at Sumatanga commented to her on the denomination's stance on civil rights: "The Methodist Church is certainly in the taillight in all this movement."[20]

Whitsett, Rutland, and Reeves were not the only north Alabama Methodists to challenge the racial status quo of the early 1950s, but few others in NAC dared to flaunt the system so directly. The blatant repression of Turnipseed's MFSA chapter and the reaction against Whitsett and Rutland from the highest quarters of church officialdom contributed to an important consequence: by the mid-1950s, liberal voices on racial issues tended to go underground. From the demise of the MFSA in 1950 throughout the rest of the decade, communications and contacts between the advocates for racial equality within the denomination were informal and unorganized. When Boston University theological student Charles Prestwood attempted to a survey Birmingham area ministers on social issues in the late 1950s, he found that many would not even respond to his anonymous questionnaire for fear that their real views might be discovered by their congregations, who then would regard the ministers as integrationists, pacifists, modernists, or Communists. Worse, they might face the possibility of harassment by White Citizens' Councils and the Klan.[21] Many Methodist clergy who might have been inclined to take a more conciliatory stance on the issue of integration found the repressive atmosphere within the conference a clear incentive to remain silent on racial matters.

Outside the state, individuals and events set in motion a reevaluation of the segregated structure in the Methodist Church—a reevaluation that the activities of a handful of clerical dissidents could not have forced. The Supreme Court decision in *Brown* challenged the Deep South's legal justification of separation of the races. On the national level, the Council of Bishops issued a statement the following November, signed by the majority of its members, endorsing the court's decision as "in harmony with the pronouncements of the Methodist Church."[22] Ironically, the newly elected president of the Council of Bishops was the Bishop of North Alabama, Clare Purcell, who stated upon his return to Birmingham that the Southeastern Jurisdiction bishops did not favor the resolution.[23] Indeed, all eight bishops of the Southeastern Jurisdiction refused to sign the statement and issued their own manifesto asserting that the racially separate jurisdictional system guaranteed blacks autonomy in administration and protected their rights and privileges as a minority.[24] But in fact, churches in the Central Jurisdiction welcomed the court's decision, and the Central Alabama Conference quickly passed a resolution praising the court for having ordered the removal of "a vicious cancer from our national life." The statement continued: "This is not the time for the blind defense of ancient prejudices, or for spiteful schemes to circumvent the law of the land. Our nation has enough lawlessness, already."[25]

For members of the two white Alabama Methodist conferences, the *Brown* decision began a decade of intense debate over the role of the church in the civil rights struggle. Alabamians in particular, faced the real possibility that segregation in all its forms might end. An issue within the church that had for the most part been ignored or suppressed now came to the forefront in a flurry of defensive statements by Southern clergy and laity. Bishop Purcell noted in the *Alabama Christian Advocate* that the statement of compliance by the national church had "no relation whatever" to its current racial organization.[26] He also recommended that no effort be made to alter a separate jurisdiction for "the colored people." The court rendered its decision prior to the 1954 annual meeting of the North Alabama Conference, and on the floor of the meeting the delegates resolved by voice vote that the jurisdictional setup should continue.[27] Lay delegate Mont Davenport, who wrote the resolution, praised "the elegant school buildings and equipment which our educational leaders have provided for our Negroes." Although Davenport in his first draft had sought to use the words "white supremacy," conference delegates balked at endorsing racism so blatantly. The resolution still received widespread support from those laity in attendance, and behind the scenes the delegates referred to Davenport as "the Kingfish"—a reference to Louisiana's former Populist governor Huey Long.[28] Davenport's resolution marked the first of many coming from Methodists in Alabama affirming segregation as a guideline for jurisdictional organization and endorsing a dual system of public education in the South.

On a local level, whites in many Southern communities responded to *Brown* by forming White Citizens' Councils committed to stopping school integration and any other attempts by the federal government to dismantle legal segregation.[29] White conservative Methodists in Alabama feared that the national church would use the end of educational segregation as a chance to force integration on annual conferences and individual churches. They had good reason for concern. By 1954 the denomination was unquestionably moving in that direction, for the General Conference had as early as 1944 appointed a national commission to study the situation of minorities in the church, with special emphasis on the Central Jurisdiction. This commission reported in 1948 and recommended more frequent interracial meetings and the establishment of a permanent office of race relations within the denomination's national administration.[30] The 1952 General Conference held an open debate over the church's racial policies that brought into question the denomination's segregated seminaries. Two years after that, the Methodist counterpart to the White Citizens' Councils in Alabama appeared in the form of a new organization that called itself the Association of Methodist Ministers and Laymen. Providing leadership for the group was the well-known Montgomery minister, G. Stanley Frazer.

Frazer had followed his father into the Methodist ministry, even though the younger man had first joined the Presbyterian Church in Georgia for about ten years. By the 1950s, he was back in the Methodist fold and leading St. James Church, one of the largest Protestant congregations in Montgomery. Frazer was known to south Alabamians as a member of a White Citizens' Council located in Selma, and he had participated in the writing of a segregationist pamphlet entitled *The Coming Tragedy*. Frazer had never been elected as a delegate to any of the General Conferences and at the age of sixty-five was not prominent in the Alabama-West Florida Conference power structure. But the 1954 *Brown* decision propelled him into a leadership role in both conferences, and he had a ready forum for his writings in the *Montgomery Advertiser*, owned by his son-in-law.[31] That summer Frazer called together a small group of laymen and ministers to devise a plan of opposition to any change or alteration of the church's racial structure. The group decided that the time was right, in the wake of *Brown*, to go on record against merging the black Central Alabama Conference into the two white Alabama conferences. With the help of local newspapers, Frazer issued an invitation for Methodists who were interested in preserving racial segregation

*A early twentieth-century view of historic Highlands Methodist Church.*

to gather at Highlands Methodist Church in Birmingham.

On December 14, 1954—seven months after *Brown* was handed down—the first meeting of Association of Methodist Ministers and Laymen convened at the Highlands church with the full support and cooperation of its pastor, Guy McGowan. Highlands was a natural venue for the meeting as it was one of the most conservative churches in the conference. Nina Reeves, a member, remembered it as the "worst of the churches; it was completely segregated."[32] McGowan energized the group by pronouncing that any attempt to "do away with all racial lines in our Church life will result in untold confusion and . . . disrupt the whole program of the Methodist Church."[33] The 275 or so assembled ministers and laymen adopted a resolution that was primarily the work of Frazer. It went on record against the integration of the jurisdictions and upheld the South's "present racial customs." As an attempt at conciliation, however, the resolution assured black Alabamians of "continued interest in their great progress as a race." A member of the association expressed a viewpoint commonly held by many white Alabamians when he reported that many of "his colored friends" had said to him, "Why don't they let us alone and let us run our own schools and churches?"[34] The Highlands meeting received attention in the local press, and Frazer himself was surprised that so many Methodists turned out for it. His appeal seemed to resonate particularly with the laity of the Alabama white conferences.

The founding of the new organization and the proceedings at the Highlands church could hardly be ignored by the conferences. In late December, R. Laurence Dill Jr., superintendent of the Birmingham district, called lay leaders of his district together and issued a statement most notable for its weakness. Their only statement of protest was an assertion that the Association of Methodist Ministers and Laymen did not officially represent the Methodist Church. But they went on to say that the Birmingham district leadership was opposed to any attempt to abolish the Central Jurisdiction.[35] In fact, the Highlands gathering had set the direction for the majority of lay Methodists in Alabama, and the local and regional Methodist hierarchy was willing to follow the laity's conservative lead. At the beginning of 1955, the bishops in the Southeastern Jurisdiction went on record as supporting the continuation of the Central Jurisdiction and argued that to include black Methodists within the white conferences would "reduce our Negro membership to a small minority . . . with less participation in the church's life and program.[36]

Despite the rhetoric, the Southeastern Jurisdiction, composed of white conferences from nine Southern states, was not numerically strong enough to control what had become a pressing social issue for Methodists nationally and internationally. By the time of the next General Conference session in Minneapolis in 1956, the civil rights struggle was well underway in the South, with Alabama itself becoming a center of civil disobedience.[37] In Minneapolis, the bishops recommended the establishment of a new study commission drawn from the church at large to evaluate the entire jurisdictional system.[38] On the floor of the assembly, delegates expressed considerable concern that Methodists were lagging behind the national pace in changing their racial policies. W. Sproule Boyd, a minister from western Pennsylvania, offered a motion that echoed the Supreme Court's *Brown* part two decision in 1955 and advocated the ending of all segregation in the Methodist Church "with reasonable speed."[39] The most important action at the 1956 General Conference was the framing of a constitutional amendment to be submitted to the annual conferences. Vaguely entitled "Amendment IX," the carefully worded document provided a plan for the gradual abolition of the Central Jurisdiction by permitting local black churches to transfer voluntarily into the white conferences. This act of union required approval by a two-thirds majority of each of the involved parties. In essence the amendment was designed to expedite the breakup of the Central Jurisdiction while seeming to preserve local white control over the pace of racial union. Central Conference leaders were generally favorable to the new procedures, but one prominent black layman warned "we are not being fooled at all by it . . . this amendment does not abolish segregation in the Methodist Church."[40]

The Minneapolis General Conference ended with the appointment of bishops in many states, including Alabama. In North Alabama, the new bishop was Bachman G. Hodge. A native of Renfro, Alabama, Hodge had spent much of his early ministry in Kentucky before the Southeastern Jurisdiction elected him to the episcopacy in 1956. At the time of his election, he was sixty-three, the oldest of the bishops elected that year, and he was not in the best of health.[41] His desire was to avoid conflict over race, and he wanted to "sit tight rather than do anything."[42] Hodge seems to have been primarily worried that talk of eliminating the Central Jurisdiction would destroy the morale of Methodist white Southerners. "This Church of ours," he wrote, "has been turned into a worried camp with many good laymen and ministers frustrated, confused and disillusioned."[43] In essence, he asked the national church for a "moratorium on mechanical changes" in the organizational structure. A measure of his own reaction to the early civil rights movement may be seen in a sharply worded letter he wrote in 1956 to Bishop G. Bromley Oxnam of Washington, D.C. Oxnam had written Hodge asking him to verify a telegram he had received from Martin Luther King Jr. that told of the city of Birmingham's jailing of the Reverend Fred Shuttlesworth and other local black leaders on vagrancy charges. Hodge's reply succinctly verified that arrests of Shuttlesworth and others had occurred, but for what he described to Oxnam as "a disturbance" on the buses.[44] Hodge regretted that "Dr. King should trouble you with this matter that has its base in the Birmingham area."

Early in 1957, the year after Hodge's arrival in Alabama, the new jurisdictional study commission held twenty-four hearings throughout the nation on the subject of jurisdictional reform. One forum occurred at G. Stanley Frazer's church in Montgomery, St. James Methodist. Some eighty Alabama Methodist laymen from both white conferences appeared before the panel. Nearly all asserted that "the Methodist Church's existence" in the South depended on the retention of the separate jurisdictions. Several interviewees warned the commissioners that abolishing the Central Jurisdiction would result in a mass walkout by "thousands of Methodists" and the reconstruction of the old Methodist Episcopal Church, South.[45] As if to drive home the point, shortly before the meeting of the next General Conference in 1960, the North Alabama Conference officially reiterated its opposition to change. Any alteration of the racial organization of Methodism, the conference told the national church, would be equivalent to breaking down "our long established custom of segregation of the races in schools, churches, and housing accommodations."[46]

Clearly many of the white Methodist laity were alarmed that the national church was moving too rapidly toward integration. The membership of the 1956 national study commission had included a number of Southerners, and one of the appointees from Montgomery provided Frazer and other Methodists with an account of the internal proceedings of the committee. Although the resulting impetus for a coalition of laity in favor of continued segregation began in south Alabama, Frazer used this information to persuade laymen and some ministers in north Alabama, especially in the Birmingham area, to take a more aggressive and organized posture on the issue. Frazer was unable to generate significant ministerial support for his segregationist strategy. But sentiment among laymen was becoming more unified against alteration of the racial divide; indeed, lay defenders of segregation were now the most powerful group within Alabama Methodism.[47]

The stimulus for increasing militancy on the part of lower South segregationists was the shift from legal challenges in the courts to black protest on the streets. In December 1955, an African American seamstress, Rosa Parks, refused to give up her seat on a Montgomery bus to a white person. Following Parks's arrest for defying local segregation ordinances, Montgomery's black community created a new organization, the Montgomery Improvement Association (MIA), and mobilized a city-wide bus boycott under the dynamic leadership of a young Baptist minister, Martin Luther King Jr. The financial dependency of the public bus system on its black ridership brought transit virtually to a halt within a year. The MIA's federal court legal challenge, citing *Brown*, to the local segregation statutes resulted in a U.S. Supreme Court affirmance in 1956 of a lower-court decision that the segregated seating law was unconstitutional.

The effectiveness of the boycott validated an approach to civil protest that became the prevailing tactic of the civil rights movement of the 1960s: nonviolent resistance with reliance on the Christian theology of forgiveness and love for one's oppressors. In Birmingham, a more militant organization, the Alabama Christian Movement for Human Rights, emerged in 1956. Created by the Reverend Fred Shuttlesworth, the ACMHR challenged the hiring practices of the city's all-white police department and demanded that the Birmingham Transit Company comply with the federal court's decision on segregated buses in the Montgomery case. Although his approach sought judicial and legal solutions to segregation, many moderate whites in Birmingham regarded Shuttlesworth as "a black analogue of the Klan."[48] His well-organized demonstrations against city authorities brought local Klan retaliation in the form of house burnings in black neighborhoods and even an attempt to kill Shuttlesworth with dynamite in his home in December 1956. The ACMHR's activities also helped motivate the re-election in the spring of 1957 of Police Commissioner Bull Connor with substantial white working class support. By the end of the decade, Shuttlesworth was confronting virtually all the segregationist city ordinances. Relations between white authorities and black activists rapidly deteriorated throughout the rest of the year and tensions continued to mount in 1958.

This was the environment in early 1959 when a group of Methodist laymen, led by two Alabama circuit judges, Whit Windham of Birmingham and L. S. Moore of Centreville, sent an unsigned invitation to every church in the two conferences for laymen to meet at Highlands Methodist Church on March 19.[49] Windham had taught the Men's Bible Class at the Highlands church for many years and local Methodists saw him as a prominent church leader. In preparation for the meeting, thirty-four laymen from both conferences signed their names to an informational booklet entitled *A Pronouncement.* The intent of the publication was clear on its cover page in that the group called themselves the Methodist Layman's Union (MLU), which was "Organized to Prevent Integrating the Church."[50] The privately financed publication was meant to provide an ideological basis for the group and to be used as a basis for discussion and action at forthcoming meetings.

A close examination of the arguments in *A Pronouncement* reveals an incongruous mix of Southern segregationist social mores and selective interpretations of Bible narratives relating to race. The real enemy was the Supreme Court and its 1954 decision implying that the South was un-Christian and even sinful. Other enemies came from within the church itself, including Methodist Church youth literature, which the pamphlet termed "propagandistic" on racial topics. The account included Emory University theology professors who had supported school desegregation, and above all, the actions of the General Conference, which were seen as forcing the integration of Methodism. The 1956 study commission came in for special criticism for its purpose was obviously to define segregation as a sin in violation of universal brotherhood. A significant portion of the booklet described the undesirable social consequences of integration within the church, especially "commingling" of the races at marriage ceremonies, hikes and swimming meets, and social functions of the Methodist Youth Fellowship. The publication at this point exhibited its most extravagant language: the "typical Negro in Alabama" was "by nature volatile and raucous." It contended that at least "sixty percent of them at a function in the Church or a private home, would render the gathering completely intolerable."[51]

In the second part of the text, the members of the MLU addressed what they believed to be the Biblical and theological foundations of segregation. Here their arguments bordered on the sophomoric. God had made the various races and purposely "placed them in separate areas on this planet." No mention was made in the ensuing text of the role of American and

The Methodist Layman's Union
(Organized to ·Prevent Integrating the Church)

☆  ☆  ☆  ☆  ☆  ☆

# A Pronouncement

*Sponsored by*
A GROUP OF METHODIST LAYMEN
*Whose Names Appear on Page 22*

☆  ☆  ☆  ☆  ☆  ☆

Laymen of Every Methodist Church Are Invited
to Join This Christian Endeavor

European slave ships in undoing the separate geographical spheres. In fact, much of the theological content was devoted to a lengthy section on the admonition of God to Abraham to protect the Israelites' racial purity, and then the Good Samaritan story was used to demonstrate that Christ never confused Christian brotherhood with true mixing of Jews and Samaritans. The theological arguments degenerated into a section on the unlikelihood that God in "his plan for human progress" would wish to "mongrelize" the "infinite life process." No breeder of stock on a Southern farm would "intentionally down breed his herds," the publication asserted; therefore "white families in the South" were just "as concerned to avoid down breeding for their children and grandchildren." The booklet's final third was devoted to another attack on *Brown*, which was claimed to be a result of the "socialist teachings of one Gunnar Myrdal."[52] (Myrdal was the Swedish sociologist who authored the pioneering 1944 study of racism in America, *An American Dilemma*). The best summary of the MLU's position came from the young theology student Charles Prestwood, who described it as a combination of the 1896 Supreme Court *Plessy v. Ferguson* decision establishing "separate but equal" with an assertion that segregation was in "harmony with the purpose and will of God."[53]

With *A Pronouncement* as their founding document, more than 1,800 laymen gathered at Highlands on the evening of March 19, 1959, and formally organized the Methodist Layman's Union. The participants included lawyers, judges, and prominent businessmen. Chair of the committee on nominations was Richard J. Stockham, the young executive of the Birmingham-based Stockham Valve and Fittings Company, and the chair of the resolutions committee was Cooper Green, vice-president of Alabama Power Company and a former mayor of Birmingham. The *Birmingham News* had reporters in attendance, and a considerable number of White Citizens' Council members attended, even though none had any official part in the program of the evening.[54] Also in attendance was the Reverend Bob Hughes, a young Methodist minister recently arrived in Alabama, who was curious about the membership of the new organization and later would become one of the MLU's most outspoken opponents.[55]

The tone of the meeting was tense given the number of known segregationists present. Judge Windham assured the audience that there was "no place" for "race agitators or Negro haters" in the proposed organization. The real purpose of the meeting, he explained, was to prevent the "breakdown" of the church as they knew it, and the first resolution passed by the group outlined that purpose: "the preservation of the jurisdictional system which keeps the Church segregated." The Methodist Layman's Union (MLU) then formed a committee of lawyers to study legal strategies that might prevent the General Conference from abolishing the jurisdictional system. Much effort was put into finding ways to elect MLU members as representatives to the 1960 General and Jurisdictional conferences, and the assembly decided to mail a slate of "approved" nominees to Methodist lay delegates to the annual meetings of the two white Alabama conferences. A few voices of dissent were heard at the gathering, most notably that of Thomas Reeves, a senior at Methodist-affiliated Birmingham-Southern College who was then serving as a supply minister at a small church south of Birmingham. "I cannot stand idly by and not speak against the propaganda included in the booklet distributed by this group," he said. To Reeves, Methodists were not purely "Anglo-Saxon," as implied by the MLU, and he deplored the organization's use of "mongrelizing the races" as a fear tactic.[56] To almost all of the assembled, however, the Highlands gathering was an important first step in saving the church from integration. As Richard Stockham put it in a report to Bishop Hodge the next day: "You would have been proud of the high level and fine spirit which filled the sanctuary."[57] He made a point of mentioning the amount of money collected in the meeting as "an amazing tribute to the earnestness of the Laymen." Thomas Reeves probably did not feel so positively about the meeting, for his church in Blue Springs promptly fired him three days after hearing of his outspokenness at the meeting.[58]

Bishop Hodge could not have been pleased with the potential impact that the organization of the Methodist Layman's Union could have on the North Alabama Conference. He wrote to Stockham and others asking them for restraint. But Hodge was also unwilling or too fearful to address their agenda publicly. When Birmingham attorney David Vann pleaded with Hodge to issue a statement disavowing any connection between the conference and the MLU, Hodge told him to talk with Windham and Green personally. Vann recollected that after having brief conversations with both men, a prominent lawyer in the Layman's Union asked him afterwards, "Are you a Communist or something?"[59] Vann then tried again to persuade Hodge that as presiding bishop he should issue a statement declaring that the movement was completely unofficial in its relation to the Methodist Church. Finally, frustrated by Hodge's inaction, he sent a mimeographed letter to many MLU leaders asking them to "exercise the highest caution and temperance in this area."[60] He told them that many of his laity and clergy friends within the church were saddened that the Layman's Union had chosen to thrust the denomination's struggles "into the glare of national publicity." Vann's own fears were related to the possibility that the Alabama church would split into warring camps over the issue of race, and he was especially disturbed by the "intemperate nature" of *A Pronouncement*'s language and the effect it would have on local black Methodists.

Ignoring all warnings, the Methodist Layman's Union wasted no time in organizing to elect its own slate of delegates to the General Conference scheduled to meet in Denver in April 1960. In late July 1959, the MLU held a rally in Decatur in which Windham told the attendees that north Alabama Methodists would send delegates to Denver "pledged to preserve our way of life."[61] He discussed at some length a bill the MLU had sponsored in the state legislature that would protect the property rights of any Protestant church that chose to pull out of a national denomination. This "Dumas Bill," sponsored by state senator Larry Dumas of Jefferson County, passed with only one dissenting vote in the Alabama house and received the unanimous support of the senate.[62] The MLU's legal committee had drawn up the proposed law after "months of study" to give local Methodist churches an escape route should the national church formally merge the black and white conferences.[63] Although the leaders of the North Alabama Conference viewed it as contrary to the denomination's property rights, the Dumas Bill was a clear warning that the conservative laity would not hesitate to break with the denomination.

By mid-1959 the Methodist Layman's Union had drawn up a list of delegates to represent its views at the 1960 General Conference. The organization's tactics were to campaign through north Alabama to firm up support for its nominees and to circulate privately a blacklist of North Alabama Conference ministers who supported combining the two white conferences with the Central Alabama Conference.[64] The MLU leaders were careful to include persons on their slate who would help them get elected, such as Dr. Henry King Stanford, president of Birmingham-Southern College and emphatically not a segregationist.[65] There was always the possibility that the MLU would alienate the lay leadership who were not supportive of its activities. Ed Montgomery, a prominent Tuscaloosa District representative on the NAC Board of Lay Activities, issued a statement strongly opposing the MLU as a group expressly organized for the purpose of electing delegates. "Do these gentlemen," he asked, expect men who have served the church for years in an official capacity to "give up this place of leadership to an outside, unauthorized group?"[66] But vocal opposition to the activities of the MLU was unusual among Methodist laity because its program was organized around the volatile issue of the national church's mandatory movement toward racial integration. Indeed, in 1960 the board of stewards of north Alabama churches in Guntersville, Roanoke, and Sylacauga joined Birmingham churches that included Bluff Park, Pleasant Grove, West End, and Birmingham First Methodist (despite the opposition of its pastor, Paul Hardin Jr.) in passing official resolutions in favor of preserving segregation within Methodist church structure.[67] West End Methodist Church leaders wrote Bishop Hodge that they wished to "affiliate" with the Methodist Layman's Union to "prevent integration in our churches."[68] When the North Alabama Conference convened in early September, the results of the MLU's careful preparation were impressive: all of the MLU's lay nominees were elected as delegates to the General Conference in Denver. The elected clerical delegates, however, also included ministers—Paul Clem, Paul Hardin Jr., Denson Franklin, and John Rutland—who had opposed the MLU's agenda and of course had not received its endorsement.[69]

This disparity between the clerical and lay delegates reveals the sharp fissures that by now existed within the North Alabama Conference. Before 1960 the Methodist clergy, with few exceptions, had chosen to downplay or ignore altogether local tension over national Methodism's proposed elimination of the Central Jurisdiction. Now the organization and prominent membership of the Methodist Layman's Union served as a warning to the clergy that powerful forces within their congregations were willing to shove ministers aside in order to preserve their churches' accustomed social order. As one layman explained, "I am not sure what the Methodist preachers think about race, but I do know that they will not defend segregation."[70]

Certainly there were Methodist clergy in Alabama who were troubled by the theological and spiritual contradictions between the segregation system and the message of Christianity. Donald Collins, a young graduate of Emory University's Candler School of Theology who entered the ministry in 1952, remembered the glaring disparity between the social environment of Alabama in the 1950s and his Candler-taught values. Indeed, his theological grounding in racial equality, Christian brotherhood, and social justice was "colliding with the reality of a totally segregated society,"[71] No Methodist minister in Alabama could escape this dilemma in the years of the civil rights movement. Joe Elmore thought that race was clearly the dominant issue facing the denomination. The racial question, Elmore believed, "was striking at the very identity of the Methodist Church; with the racial thing we were dealing with our very being."[72] Those who believed like Elmore that "racism was an all pervasive cancer" in the church and society were more representative of the younger generation of clergy. But all Methodist clergy in Alabama had to confront one unpleasant reality: they had to maintain their professional security in a denomination that, by virtue of its hierarchical organization, could end its segregation by a mandate from the General Conference. Then they as ministers of that national body would be charged with the responsibility of desegregating their annual conferences and even their local churches. Before this eventuality, it was in the interest of ministers to maintain silence on the issue lest they arouse the wrath of their congregations. To speak out on behalf of integration was to risk professional ruin and the probability that one should begin looking for a post outside Alabama. This in fact had happened to Andrew Turnipseed, who had gone to a Rochester, New York, church, and Dan Whitsett, who was by now in a Boston church near Harvard University where he was to spend the next decade.[73]

Bishop Hodge had readily arranged the transfer of Turnipseed to upper state New York. He was reluctant to confront the activism that was emerging in his conference, and his leadership style was symptomatic of the difficulties that nearly all Southern bishops encountered as the civil rights movement intensified by the end of the 1950s. The bishop's letters and policy announcements from 1956 to 1961 indicate that he was extremely troubled by the racial question within and outside the church. Hodge tended to appoint district superintendents whom he could trust not to be radical or aggressively liberal.[74] To a request from a Christian education worker that he appoint a black minister to a Methodist commission on education, Hodge replied that he recognized the need that attention be paid to coordination with black Methodists' education programs, but at the "present time, the tension is so great that it is difficult to maintain communications."[75]

Sunday School education programs posed a particularly troublesome problem for Hodge. Within his own episcopacy, local congregations inundated Hodge with complaints about the integrated scenes in church literature issued by Abington Press, the Methodist publishing house in Nashville, Tennessee. Whites objected to scenes of integrated groups of school-age children, and even a picture depicting a black pastor serving communion to two black children aroused protests. The content of the articles was also under attack, and a Wylam, Alabama, church objected strongly to a characterization of Martin Luther King Jr. as a leader who demonstrated "a spirit of love and nonviolence."[76] The board of stewards of Birmingham's white Central Methodist Church wrote Hodge that the Methodist youth publications seemed "hipped on the subject of segregation in the South" and followed a line that closely approached communism in many cases.[77] Hodge's approach to such controversies was to ask Abingdon Press to respond directly. The head of its editorial division, Henry M. Bullock, usually complied. One memorandum to a commission on education at Lake Highlands Methodist Church is typical of Bullock's approach to these attacks from local churches. He explained that he was aware of difficulties in present racial relations, but the church's publications were based "firmly on the teachings of Jesus Christ" and the Methodist *Discipline.* Bullock seemed to backtrack somewhat in the second part of his letter by assuring the local commission that none of the literature emanating from Nashville promoted the idea of interracial marriages or the abolition of the Central Jurisdiction.[78] Many Methodist Christian educators in the two white conferences chose to stop using Methodist literature and to use instead substitutes from the Southern Baptists or Presbyterians.

As Hodge contemplated the upcoming 1960 General Conference in Denver, the daily correspondence on his desk represented wide disagreement within his own conference over the future of the church and race. Prominent in his files in 1959 were resolutions from area churches in north Alabama giving strong support to the Methodist Layman's Union. The board of stewards at Decatur's Central Methodist Church put it simply: "We believe, as we think most Southern Methodists do, white and colored, in the segregation of the two races. We consciously feel that there is nothing wrong with it."[79] The *Birmingham News* reported on most of these resolutions in some detail, and they echoed the admonition of the Bluff Park parishioners to the bishop that any movement toward integration at Denver would not only be "disastrous and un-Christian" but would split the church forever.[80] Such predictions of institutional disaster thrust Hodge into lethargy and depression as the Denver meeting approached.

## NOTES

1.  Joe Elmore interview tape by Mitch Robinson, June 6, 2001, NACA.
2.  Quoted in Bass, *Blessed Are the Peacemakers*, 22.
3.  Robert L. Wilson., *Methodists and Foreign Policy since World War II*, (http://www.cmpage.org/biasese/chapter2.html).
4.  Prestwood, "Social Ideas," 296, 299.
5.  Stanley High, "Methodism's Pink Fringe," *Readers Digest*, vol. 56, February 1950, 134–138.
6.  Wilson, *Methodists and Foreign Policy.*
7.  *Alabama Christian Advocate*, February 7, 1950.
8.  Ibid., October 24, 1950.
9.  William C. Davis interview tape, May 9, 2001, Robinson, NACA.
10. Interview with Ray Goodwin by William Nicholas, September 21, 2002.
11. Paul Hardin to Bachman G. Hodge, February 18, 1958, NACA 6.3, Bishops' Papers.
12. Davis Interview tape, May 9, 2001, Robinson, NACA.
13. John Rutland. *Mary and Me: Telling the Story of Prevenient Grace* (Pensacola: Adara House, 1996), 106, 107. The stories of Connor's interruptions of Rutland's sermons have been disputed, but in an interview with a church member from the time I corroborated Rutland's account.
14. John Rutland interview, Nicholas, February 22, 1996.
15. Rutland, *Mary and Me*, 111.
16. Ibid.
17. Joe Elmore interview tape, April 6, 2001, Robinson, NACA.
18. Joe Elmore interview, May 8, 2002, Nicholas.
19. The Wesley Foundation is a United Methodist ministry begun in 1913 and sponsored by the church as an outreach program on non-church-owned and -operated college and university campuses.
20. Nina Reeves interview tape, April 15, 2001, Robinson, NACA.
21. Prestwood, "Social Ideas," 341, 402.
22. *Alabama Christian Advocate*, November 30, 1954.
23. The Council of Bishops consisted of all bishops currently serving in the six jurisdictions of the Methodist Church. The Southeastern Jurisdiction included Mississippi, Alabama, Georgia, Florida, North and South Carolina, Tennessee, Kentucky, and Virginia.

24. *Statement from College of Bishops*, Southeast Jurisdiction of the Methodist Episcopal Church, NACA, 1954.

25. "Statement and Resolution to the Central Alabama Conference," *Central Alabama Conference Journal,* 79.

26. *Alabama Christian Advocate*, November 30, 1954.

27. Ibid., October 5, 1954. *Peter C. Murray's Methodists and the Crucible of Race* (Columbia, Missouri, University of Missouri Press, 2004) maintains that white Americans believed in two myths that the *Brown* decision confronted and threatened: first, that racial progress was occurring in the United States and could be solved by existing institutions and organizations, and secondly within the American South a conviction that any change in race relations could only come gradually and under the direction of the existing white power structure. Murray sees the Methodist Church as an institution caught between the first nationwide "Great Myth" and the second "Southern Myth" that served to justify a segregated social order within the church (pp. 79–80).

28. Davis interview tape, May 9, 2001, Robinson, NACA.

29. The Citizens' Councils, sometimes called the "white-collar Klan," were mainly comprised of middle-class whites who tried to control blacks through economic reprisals (depriving activist blacks of jobs, mortgages, and credit) rather than outright violence.

30. *Journal of the General Conference of the Methodist Church , 1948* (Nashville: Methodist Publishing House, 1948), 461, 735.

31. Prestwood, "Social Issues," 345, 357, 364.

32. Reeves interview tape, May 7, 2001, Robinson, NACA.

33. *Alabama Christian Advocate*, December 7, 1954.

34. Prestwood, "Social Ideas, 350, 247.

35. *Alabama Christian Advocate,* December 21, 1954.

36. Ibid., February 15, 1955.

37. The Montgomery bus boycott began on Monday, December 5, 1955, led by the local NAACP and the new young pastor of the Dexter Avenue Baptist Church, Martin Luther King Jr.

38. The official title of the group was "The Commission to Study and Recommend Action Regarding Jurisdictional Relations," but the group was known within Methodist ranks as the "Commission of Seventy."

39. In May of 1955, the U.S. Supreme Court issued what became known as *Brown II*, ordering that desegregation of schools proceed with "all deliberate speed."

40. 1956 General Conference *Journal*, 412, 471. The Supreme Court in 1955 had used the words "all deliberate speed." The amendment was obviously worded to give the Southern bishops the leeway to say to their conferences that Southern control over the denomination's composition would be preserved indefinitely. The action was an implicit recognition of the importance of the South in the Methodist order in terms of church membership and influence.

41. Davis interview tape, May 9, 2001, Robinson, NACA.

42. Ibid.

43. Memorandum, n.d., NACA 6.3, Bishops' Papers.

44. Hodge to G. Bromley Oxnam, November 5, 1958, ibid.

45. *Alabama Christian Advocate,* October 29, 1957.

46. Ibid., September 22, 1959.

47. Prestwood, "Social Ideas, 365, 366.

48. J. Mills Thornton III, *Dividing Lines: Municipal Politics and the Struggle for Civil Rights in Birmingham, Montgomery, and Selma* (Tuscaloosa: University of Alabama Press, 2002), 203. For an account of Shuttlesworth's civil rights career, see Andrew Michael Manis, *A Fire You Can't Put Out: The Civil Rights Life of Birmingham's Reverend Fred Shuttlesworth* (Tuscaloosa: University of Alabama Press, 1999).

49. *Birmingham News,* March 4, 1959.

50. Methodist Layman's Union, *A Pronouncement* (Birmingham, Alabama: Methodist Layman's Union, 1959).

51. Ibid., 7, 8.

52. Ibid., 10–17.

53. Prestwood, "Social Ideas," 373–381, *passim.*

54. Ibid., 368.

55. Bob Hughes was officially a "minister under special appointment." This meant that he had been appointed by the bishop to serve in some capacity other than a pastor or district superintendent. In this instance, Hughes was working in an administrative role with the Alabama Council on Human Relations, an affiliate of the Southern Regional Council, a biracial Atlanta-based organization started during the Progressive Era to crusade against lynching and to improve black-white relations in the South. Hughes's activities in Alabama would soon make him a controversial figure.

56. *Birmingham News,* March 20, 1959.

57. Richard J. Stockham to Bachman G. Hodge, March 20, 1959, NACA 6.3, Bishops' Papers. Bachman Hodge had replaced Clare Purcell as North Alabama's bishop in 1956 after Purcell retired at the age of seventy-two.

58. William Hitt to Hodge, March 25, 1959, NACA 6.3, Bishops' Papers.

59. Vann interview tape, May 21, 2001, Robinson, NACA. Thomas Reeves continued his civil rights activism. He was arrested as a result of his participation in sit-ins in 1960 and was ordered confined to the Birmingham-Southern campus for his own safety (Donald Brown, *Forward, Forever, Birmingham-Southern College at Its Sesquicentennial* (Birmingham: Birmingham-Southern College, 2005), 182.

60. Vann to Members of the Layman's Union, March 12, 1959, NACA 6.3, Bishops' Papers.

61. *Birmingham News,* July 31, 1959.

62. Ibid., August 12, 1959.

63. Ed Montgomery interview tape, April 11, 2001, Robinson, NACA.

64. Tillman Sprouse to Ed Montgomery, April 21, 1959, NACA 74, Montgomery Papers.

65. Montgomery interview tape, Robinson. NACA. Henry King Stanford consistently defended the right of Birmingham-Southern students to participate in civil rights activities, and he resigned his presidency in 1962 after verbal attacks on him by Bull Connor and other racists made his trustees increasingly non-supportive.

66. "Statement," Ed Montgomery, August 2, 1959, in NACA 74, Montgomery Papers.

67. Resolutions, Bishops Papers, 1959, NACA 6.3, Bishops' Papers.

68. Board of Stewards of West End Methodist Church to Hodge, April 6, 1959, ibid.

69. *Alabama Christian Advocate*, September 22, 1959.

70. Quoted in Prestwood, "Social Ideas," 394.

71. Donald Collins, *When the Church Bell Rang Racist: The Methodist Church and Civil Rights in Alabama* (Macon, Georgia, 2005), 14.

72. Elmore interview with Nicholas, March 1, 1996, NACA.

73. Andrew Turnipseed had openly participated in a bus integration movement in Mobile and Bishop Hodge secured a pastoral appointment for him in Rochester to get him out of Alabama.

74. Davis interview tape, May 9, 2001, Robinson, NACA.

75. Hodge to Mrs. Clytie May Thomas, January 20, 1959, NACA 6.3, Bishops' Papers.

76. Resolution of Martin Memorial Methodist Church, n.d., ibid.

77. Board of Stewards of Central Methodist Church to Hodge, May 12, 1958, ibid.

78. Henry M. Bullock to Lake Highlands Methodist Church, January 28, 1958, ibid.

79. Central Methodist Church to Hodge, n.d., ibid.

80. *Birmingham News*, February 17, 1959.

# II.

# Days of Crisis, 1960–1964

As Bishop Hodge and his conference prepared for the 1960 General Conference meeting in Denver, the tempo of civil rights protests was accelerating throughout the South.

The success of the Montgomery bus boycott had motivated a group of black ministers, convened by the Reverend Dr. Martin Luther King Jr. in early 1957, to form the Southern Christian Leadership Conference as an alliance of local organizations committed to working against Jim Crow segregation. King served as its president, and in 1960 he resigned as pastor of Montgomery's Dexter Avenue Baptist Church and moved his family to Atlanta, his hometown and where SCLC was headquartered. King and his chief lieutenant, fellow Baptist minister Ralph Abernathy, traveled widely to spread the strategy of nonviolent direct action against segregation.

Meanwhile, a group of college and seminary students in Nashville had been studying and practicing Gandhian-inspired techniques of passive resistance as a mechanism for challenging segregation. Their preparation for a campaign of civil rights demonstrations was preempted when four black students in North Carolina spontaneously sat-in at a lunch counter on February 1, 1960. That action launched the sit-in movement and soon led to the formation of the Student Nonviolent Coordinating Committee (SNCC), which along with SCLC and the Congress of Racial Equality (CORE) would be the primary groups ushering in a new wave of activism that lasted through most of the 1960s. The result, of course, was the sweeping away of legalized segregation in the South, though not without tremendous struggle, conflict, and violence.

In the Deep South, most white college campuses were slow to show evidence of the new student activism, including Birmingham-Southern College where the North Alabama Conference held its annual meeting in the fall of

1959. As the most important of the three Methodist colleges in Alabama, both in terms of academic standards and enrollment, Birmingham-Southern provided a comfortable atmosphere for delegates to socialize between sessions, and a good many important decisions were made beneath the shady trees on its stately grounds.[1] The yearly meetings of the annual conferences represented to many Methodists the most important event in the church calendar. There the leadership voted on constitutional amendments then before the national church, elected delegates to the General Conference, and determined matters relating to ordination, character, and conference relations of ministers.

Conference ministers and delegates elected from the various congregations comprised the membership of the Annual Conference. Although most of the sessions were devoted to mundane reports from the various boards and agencies of the conference plus the usual wrangling over budgets for the upcoming year, excitement mounted when the ministerial appointments to the various churches were announced. This was where strong personalities emerged. In the weeks leading up to the conferences, ambitious young ministers sought to move on to larger churches while the lay representatives of individual congregations tried to get the bishop to appoint a new preacher for their locales. As one commentator on the structure of the Methodist polity explained, the annual meeting was meant to be a real exercise in "participatory democracy."[2]

The future of the Central Alabama Conference was a topic of much discussion at the 1959 gathering. With the blessing of Bishop Hodge, the assembly passed a resolution written by two of its best known and highly respected delegates, who would be going to the General Conference in Denver: the Reverend Laurence Dill of Anniston and BSC President Dr. Henry King Stanford. The document endorsed the status quo and argued that to change the jurisdictional system would jeopardize "the union" of the church.[3] This position was unacceptable to the most enthusiastic supporters of integration, but it represented a compromise that the NAC could support and send as a memorial to the General Conference.[4] Bishop Hodge himself was hoping that the 1956 Amendment IX, which allowed for voluntary transfers of churches, would avoid forced racial integration.[5]

In Denver the following May, however, the Methodist General Conference "steamrolled" (as the *Birmingham News* characterized it) over the Southern delegations in endorsing the recommendations of the Commission of Seventy to move ahead with the union of the jurisdictions.[6] The General Conference carefully used the word "merger" instead of "integration" or "racial union." But semantics made no difference to the delegates from the white Alabama conferences. They were in the minority. Even though they voted solidly against the commission's report and opposed it on the floor, the General Conference went on record on April 28, 1960, as overwhelmingly favoring the elimination of the black Central Jurisdiction.[7] The stage was thereby set for a confrontation between white conferences in the South and the national church. A further resolution, which proposed giving the national church authority to transfer bishops across state lines and to consecrate them at General Conference gatherings, underscored the denomination's determination to destroy the segregated structure of the Methodist Church.

The bitterness of the Southerners' defeat in Denver was unmitigated by the fact that the delegates returned to a state and region on the brink of a social revolution. In Greensboro, North Carolina in 1960, four black freshmen at North Carolina A&T State University sat down at a whites-only lunch counter and stayed until local police arrested them. The Greensboro sit-in inspired thousands of black and some white students from schools inside and outside the South to stage sit-ins in dozens of cities and spurred the creation of SNCC. At the same time, SCLC was becoming more politically strategic in selecting areas of protest. Birmingham, a city dominated by a reactionary and racist police chief and rigidly segregated by local law and custom, was clearly an attractive target for King's activities. The Reverend Fred Shuttlesworth, an SCLC co-founder and the creator and leader of the Birmingham-based Alabama Christian Movement for Human Rights, urged King to come to the city not only to give the movement "prestige [but] really shake the country."[8]

In 1960 a young *New York Times* reporter, Harrison Salisbury, traveled to Birmingham to investigate racial conditions in the city. His two-part report in the *Times* in April 1960 powerfully indicted Birmingham's white political and social establishment. According to Salisbury, the "emotional dynamite of racism" had completely destroyed the possibility of a "reasoned approach" to the city's civic problems. His article detailed the almost complete segregation of public facilities. Whites and blacks walked on the same streets, Salisbury wrote, but other than utilize the same water supply and sewer system, that was about all they did together. Blacks and whites were not allowed to use the same ballparks, taxicabs, and libraries. The reporter's five-day stay convinced him that "every channel of communication, every medium of mutual interest, every reasoned approach, every inch of middle ground has been fragmented." Salisbury concluded that this environment had created a community of fear, reinforced by the harsh repressive hand of the police and the uncontrolled violence perpetrated by local segregationist groups like the KKK.[9]

Birmingham's future was simply bleak. Both Birmingham newspapers denounced the Salisbury article, and city officials filed a defamation suit against Salisbury and the *Times* claiming that he had libeled their community and its leaders.[10] In an unexpected way, the Salisbury articles also affected the North Alabama Conference, as one of its ministers was pulled into the uproar and backlash which followed their publication.

Among the few biracial groups working towards improved race relations in the state in the 1950s and '60s was the Alabama Council on Human Relations (ACHR), an affiliate of the Atlanta-based Southern Regional Council. The biracial SRC, started as part of the Progressive-era crusade against lynching, had served since 1919 as a channel of communication between whites and blacks in the segregated South. Throughout the 1940s and '50s the SRC gathered information about the Ku Klux Klan and other racist hate groups nationwide. ACHR consisted of no more than three hundred members, about half of them black, who usually met once a year on the campuses of black colleges to discuss their program for the coming year.[11] In 1954 the Alabama Council named as its new executive secretary Bob Hughes, a native of Gadsden and a recent graduate of Emory University's Candler School of Theology.

Bishop Clare Purcell allowed Hughes to have what was known as "an appointment beyond the local church" as head of the ACHR. Hughes was a soft-spoken, slightly built young minister who originally had wanted to be a missionary in Africa.[12] Once he was working for the SRC, he demonstrated great energy and commitment. He was quite naturally interested in the segregationist movement in his own church and filed several reports with the main SRC office in Atlanta that emphasized the amount of private money behind the anti-merger forces in Methodism.[13]

Hughes had been on the Birmingham scene in late 1959 when the Methodist Layman's Union was organized, and his reports in the *Alabama Council Newsletter* provided valuable insights into the mentality and social background of its members. Hughes described the average participant as middle-aged, older, and reasonably well-dressed. Hughes again mentioned the money that seemed to be behind the MLU, whose leaders included prominent businessmen and lawyers. He did not underestimate the impact that mobilization of lay influence would have on the denomination. "If the Layman's Union could muster 1200 people . . . at a time of relative calm," he wrote, "what kind of response could be aroused again when Birmingham is wracked with school desegregation."[14] Hughes had close personal ties with black leadership in Alabama because the ACHR was a biracial organization. His newsletter recorded the frustration that black Methodists experienced with the formation of the MLU. "I can't express what it's done to me," one Central Alabama Conference pastor told Hughes. "I've almost said I'm sorry I'm a Methodist," the pastor continued. "If I were a few years younger, I'd probably transfer to another denomination."[15] Hughes was forceful in warning the white conferences that if merger succeeded then the MLU leadership was planning to withdraw from the national denomination and reestablish the old Methodist Episcopal Church, South.

The Methodist Layman's Union leadership was not long in responding to what they regarded as Hughes's personal attack in the *Alabama Council Newsletter*, which many Methodist ministers had received in the mail. Whit Windham, who had helped organize the Highlands meeting of the MLU, issued a press statement in May 1959 that identified the Alabama Council on Human Relations as a small biracial group preaching full racial integration on all levels of the denomination.[16] Windham labeled the *Newsletter* as "propaganda" on the part of Hughes who, according to the MLU, was attacking the very "laymen . . . who provide the funds and homes for retired ministers in which he [Hughes] will share on retirement." After Windham's attack, a cavalcade of Klansmen came by Hughes's home and burned a six-foot cross in his front yard. His friend Charles "Chuck" Morgan described Hughes as victimized by what an attorney friend described as "local smear-sheet artists, late-night telephone callers, and other merchants of hate."[17]

Hughes was an important source for any journalist wishing to know more about the racial situation in Alabama, and Harrison Salisbury had interviewed him for some of the information on which he based his *Times* reports. Following the *Times* publication of the Salisbury article, city investigators were able to obtain telephone numbers of Salisbury's outgoing calls from the Tutwiler Hotel, where Salisbury had stayed. Hughes's number was among those listed. A grand jury in Bessemer began an investigation into whether Salisbury had committed "criminal libel" in defaming the city and its leaders and ordered Hughes to appear and to bring with him official records from the Alabama Council on Human Relations.[18] Materials specified in Hughes's summons included office memoranda, cancelled checks, and correspondence showing all contributions and donations made since 1958. The real object of the grand jury had less to do with Salisbury than with obtaining a list of ACHR supporters. The release of this information would have revealed to the jury the names of important financial supporters of the council in the Birmingham area, including Avondale Mills and businessmen Donald Comer and Mervyn H. Stern.[19] Hughes feared that compliance with the grand jury could jeopardize not only his contributors and members but also threaten the council's existence.[20] David Vann, one of Hughes's Methodist friends and a former law clerk to U.S. Supreme Court Justice Hugo Black, told him that the prosecution for criminal libel against Salisbury was unconstitutional and in fact had last been used in seventeenth-century England against political opponents of the government.[21] Hughes decided to hire his very able friend Chuck Morgan to defend him and then to answer before the grand jury only those questions that directly concerned his conversations with Salisbury. He refused to furnish any information that would compromise the internal records of the ACHR.

When Hughes appeared before the grand jury on September 2, his refusal to comply with their subpoena for council documents brought him a citation for contempt of the court. Bessemer authorities then arrested and jailed Hughes. Morgan went immediately to see him and supplied a bottle of milk for Hughes's chronic ulcers and a copy of John F. Kennedy's *Profiles in Courage*.[22] Morgan later recalled that he received phone calls from a number of Methodist ministers the evening that Hughes went to jail. Among the callers was Hughes's friend John Rutland who, upon hearing the news, called his district superintendent, R. E. Kimbrough, and Bishop Hodge to urge them to intervene. Both men claimed to be too busy on the grounds that the annual meeting of the North Alabama Conference was to start the next day. So Rutland and his young associate pastor, Frank Dawson, without assistance from their superiors, went to bail Hughes out of jail.[23] They failed in this attempt, but they were able to send a note of encouragement up to the imprisoned minister. Suddenly and without explanation, Hughes was released on September 6. He was surprised because he obviously was in contempt of the court by refusing to hand over his records. He concluded that Bessemer authorities realized the potential for unfavorable nationwide publicity if they kept him in jail.[24] The following week the grand jury issued another subpoena to Hughes, but this time without mention of financial records or membership lists. A few days later Hughes appeared before the Bessemer authorities and testified about his conversations with Salisbury. The grand jury ultimately indicted Salisbury on forty-two counts of criminal libel. But the reporter was back in New York City by then and the indictment was never served.

Hughes's own days in Alabama were numbered. He was convinced that the Methodist Layman's Union was behind his indictment: a lawyer on the circuit court staff was a member of the Bessemer First Methodist Church and the Layman's Union. Hughes also thought that the MLU was responsible for the subsequent decision by the NAC's Council on Ministries to recommend that he resign his post with the Alabama Council on Human Relations and accept a new assignment.[25] While Bishop Hodge accepted this committee recommendation, friends of Hughes moved quickly to help him achieve his longtime desire to be a missionary in Africa. The Methodist bishop of southern Rhodesia, Ralph E. Dodge, was receptive and invited Hughes to come there to do missionary work. Two days later the NAC quickly approved his transfer to Rhodesia. Hughes himself by this time was quite willing to leave Alabama, and from Rhodesia he later wrote his lawyer of his state of mind as he left the state. "I remember so well," he wrote, "driving home alone the afternoon I was removed from the ministry." Passing through the Birmingham neighborhood of Southside, he saw a small black boy playing in a gutter and thought that if there was the slightest chance that his own work in Alabama had made the youngster's future brighter, then "the opposition didn't really matter—the acceptance or rejection of others was not nearly as important as whether or not I had done my best."[26] Morgan's own thoughts were that Hughes was forced to pay a high price for his Christian principles in a community that called itself a "city of churches."[27]

Consideration of the Hughes case was one of the last worries faced by Bachman Hodge, who died after a lengthy hospital stay in January of 1961. Nolan B. Harmon replaced Hodge as bishop of the North Alabama Conference. Harmon was a Mississippi-born minister who had studied at Emory University's Candler School of Theology, earned a master's degree from Princeton, and represented the third generation of Methodist preachers in his family. He was a divine of the old school. His theology was centered on salvation from personal sin—and not on the social gospel.[28] True to his Mississippi origins, Harmon had romanticized the Old South, often preaching sermons on Robert E. Lee during his early ministry. In 1956 the Southeast Jurisdiction elected him bishop. His reputation was that of a Southerner who defended the segregated jurisdictional system both in writing and on the floor of the General Conference. Harmon made a speech at the 1956 General Conference in which he argued that defense of a minority was the real reason for jurisdictional separation of black and white Methodists.[29] In fact, much of the support for Harmon's elevation to the episcopacy came from the laity of the Southeastern Jurisdiction who saw him as a staunch defender of the status quo in race relations.[30] When Harmon was given his post in the North Alabama Conference, he was already bishop of the Western North Carolina Conference, so in effect he was given two conferences to superintend. The bishop chose not to live in Birmingham on any permanent basis and made the Tutwiler Hotel his Alabama home while he shuttled between his two bishoprics. Many Alabamians thought of Harmon as an "absentee" bishop, and he did rely on two able district superintendents in Birmingham, Jack Edgar and Tillman Sprouse, to administer the NAC during his prolonged periods of absence.[31] Harmon was not inclined at first to devote much time to learning about his new conference. One layman recalled that when Harmon was working on ministerial appointment for an upcoming meeting, he had to choose ministers for Phil Campbell, a small northwest Alabama town. Harmon mistook the place for a person and asked his cabinet, "Who is Phil Campbell?"[32] No one found the bishop to be anything less than kindly in demeanor, well-dressed, and knowledgeable about the history of Methodism. Many perceived him to have the mind of a church scholar, and he did have an impressive record of publications. The Reverend Duncan Hunter, who served in Harmon's cabinet, found the new bishop to be a very bookish person, "a kind and loving gentleman and not an activist."[33] He was also a man of significant experience within the church, being nearly seventy when he came to Birmingham. Although Harmon's tenure in Alabama might be regarded as an "interim" appointment to fill the remainder of Hodge's term, he came to the state at a crucial juncture in the merger struggle and presided through two tumultuous years of civil rights strife in Birmingham.

Race was not an issue in which Harmon had much interest, and his formative years in Mississippi had led him to deplore social strife.[34] He found to his dismay that Alabama was undergoing considerable turmoil over the segregation system. Conditions in the North Alabama Conference were going to require more of his time and attention than he had expected.[35] Harmon was shocked by state patrolmen displaying Confederate flags on their cars and using their dogs to frighten people. But his heart was not in merger. During a 1961 address in North Carolina, Harmon commented that if an African American came to his church and asked for membership, he would ask if he came to "worship or to demonstrate."[36] If the motivation were simply to "break down racial barriers that our social mores has established for generations," then Harmon would direct him to join an all-black congregation.

North Alabama Methodists recognized that Harmon was a gradualist on race after his reaction to the beginning of Freedom Rider episodes in Birmingham.

On Mother's Day, May 14, 1961, a Trailways bus pulled into the downtown Birmingham bus terminal with a small integrated group of civil rights activists aboard. The activists, who came to be known as freedom riders, were traveling from Washington, D.C., to New Orleans, Louisiana, to test the enforcement of recent Interstate Commerce Commission rules prohibiting segregation in interstate bus travel. The activists had already been attacked in other locations and their impending arrival in Birmingham was expected. Waiting in Birmingham was a mob of Klansmen whom the police allowed to assault the riders in a bloody attack as horrified news reporters and others looked on. Police Commissioner Bull Connor not only removed his officers from the scene but permitted his headquarters to inform the Klan as to when the bus would arrive at the Trailways terminal.[37] Earlier that day Connor's pastor at Woodlawn Methodist, John Rutland, had pleaded with him to protect the riders on the bus, but Connor as usual ignored Rutland. The attacks on the bus passengers and innocent bystanders ended only after the Birmingham police showed up conveniently late. Connor subsequently claimed that he had inadequate police personnel that day because so many of his men wanted to be at home with their mothers.[38]

As the North Alabama Conference prepared to convene its annual session on the campus of Birmingham-Southern College in late May 1961, the state was a tinderbox of racial tension. At a press conference after the attacks on the bus riders, Governor John Patterson had told reporters that he had no sympathy for the freedom riders, and he refused to take calls from President John F. Kennedy on the situation.[39] In mid-May a mob in Montgomery attacked a Greyhound bus bearing more freedom riders, including some of the ones beaten earlier in Birmingham. The rioting by whites that ensued was quelled only after U.S. Attorney General Robert Kennedy sent in federal marshals and Patterson finally declared martial law and dispatched National Guardsmen.

The Methodist establishment began to take official notice of the rapidly deteriorating situation in the state. *The Alabama Christian Advocate* editorialized that the Sunday calm of May 14 had been suddenly shattered

*John Rutland, center, chairing a meeting at Woodlawn Methodist Church in the early 1960s.*

by "the strident cries of a savage mob viciously attacking helpless victims." The *Advocate* concluded that the freedom riders had a right to come to Alabama and that the attacks upon them were "inexcusable, unlawful and deserving of swift punishment." [40] Bishop Harmon devoted a major part of his opening conference address to the same subject, but his own white traditionalist point of view emerged in his assertion that there had been a "sudden assault by vast outside powers crashing into the mores and long-established customs of a great people." The result had been what the bishop labeled "mob violence." He went on to say that even though the South had not treated blacks fairly, integration would only be achieved "by the slow, slow, slow process of time." Joe Elmore, who attended the conference, was particularly struck by the rhetorical emphasis that Harmon placed on the repetition of the word "slow." Although he thought that most NAC delegates were sympathetic to what the bishop was saying, he also believed that the delegates showed a naïve assumption that racial inclusion in the South could come through voluntary action. [41]

Despite the bishop's defensive words, one important Birmingham church had already begun to shift away from the belief that important changes in race relations could be put off to future generations. The Reverend Paul Hardin had steadfastly opposed bigotry and the concept of white superiority during his eleven-year tenure as pastor of First Methodist Church in downtown Birmingham before being elevated to the episcopacy in 1960.[42] Although Hardin knew that many in his congregation disagreed with him, he had welcomed all who entered the doors of First Methodist. He instructed his ushers that they should not turn away black visitors. After 1960, Hardin headed the Alabama-West Florida Conference. To replace him at Birmingham's First Methodist, Bishop Harmon had chosen Denson Franklin, who had been at Gadsden First Methodist for fourteen years.

The appointment in Birmingham was somewhat of a surprise to Franklin himself, for normally the ministers who served at the 4,500-member church came from outside the conference.[43] Harmon probably chose Franklin as the right man to go to Birmingham's leading congregation because he had a reputation for dealing with controversial external events with diplomacy and moderation. Franklin's skill was perhaps first displayed in labor relations when he helped to settle a serious dispute between the Goodyear Tire Company and its Gadsden employees in the 1950s. His viewpoint on racial division was clear: he wanted the power of "love and mercy" to bring about the integration of the church in Alabama. At the same time, Franklin believed that it would take "patience to work out the racial issue." His approach, whether dealing with his conservative church members or those whom he described as "more progressive," would best be described as "moderation."[44] Franklin quickly made contact with other like-minded ministers in the city, chief among them Rabbi Milton Grafman of Temple Emmanuel.[45] On the issue of conservative lay organizations, Franklin was perhaps most aggressive. He fought off attempts by the MLU to influence his congregation, maintaining that church membership at First Methodist must always have an "open door" to anyone who wished to attend. He began to have the reputation throughout the North Alabama Conference as a minister who had the personal skills to communicate with both sides in racial controversies.

Franklin found, much to his surprise, that there was a precedent for integration at First Methodist. Three or four black families already were longtime members of the church; they sat in the balcony at Sunday services. However, one side effect of the freedom riders episode was that Franklin's few black members stopped coming to church.

During 1962, tension built in the city with the municipal authorities closing nearly all segregated public facilities to slow demonstrations and growing black support for a boycott of downtown stores.[46] Businessmen, led by Birmingham Chamber of Commerce President Sidney Smyer, began a political reform movement to bypass Bull Connor by replacing the three-man city commission with a new mayor/city council form of government. The new mayor could then directly control the police department and remove Connor. Even though the reform process went forward and the city gained a new mayor, Albert Boutwell, and city council by the spring of the following year, Connor refused to leave his post as police commissioner. He created chaos with a lengthy court challenge seeking to serve out the remainder of his term. In effect, Birmingham had two city governments at the same time.[47]

This was the confusing political setting for the SCLC's major civil rights offensive that began in April 1963. Martin Luther King Jr. and SCLC associates made downtown Birmingham businesses the focus of "Project C"—the C stood for *Confrontation*. However, important persons among the white moderates and the black business establishment (significantly, millionaire insurance titan A. G. Gaston) wanted King to delay his protest until the new mayor-council government was firmly in control and had been given a chance to prove that the new regime of white officials could compromise.[48] Prominent church leaders were among the white moderates, and Bishop Harmon joined other local clergy in forming a group that met periodically to discuss the racial situation in the city and state. In the beginning, this was more a luncheon group than anything more formal, and it included the Methodist bishop from the Alabama-West Florida Conference, Paul Hardin, Episcopal bishops C. C. J. Carpenter and coadjutor George Murray, Roman Catholic Bishop Joseph A. Durick, Rabbi Milton Grafman, the Reverend Earl Stallings of Birmingham First Baptist Church, and Dr. Edward V. Ramage of the Birmingham First Presbyterian Church. Harmon was new to Alabama but he took an active role in helping organize meetings of the group.

The church leaders had hoped that Bull Connor's defeat in the April

2 mayoral election would result in King's canceling plans to protest in Birmingham. Toward this end, the clergymen wrote a joint letter to King requesting that "all agitation be held up," thereby allowing time to "smooth things out."[49] Although Harmon later often took credit for initiating the meeting that occurred in his hotel room on Good Friday, April 12, Rabbi Grafman actually drafted the letter, with suggestions from the assembled clergymen.[50] The statement signed by all the ministers appeared in the *Birmingham News* and the *Birmingham Post-Herald* the next day, and it was straightforward in its assertion that King's demonstrations would be "unwise and untimely." The clergymen essentially took issue with King's strategy of nonviolent protest. They believed such a strategy would incite "hatred and violence" and make the situation worse in the city. Perhaps the most incongruous part of the letter was its inclusion of a statement of commendation that the local news media and law enforcement officials had handled the demonstrations "in a calm manner." The Good Friday statement ended by asking blacks and whites to display "law and order and common sense."[51] This letter's publication came only one day after King's arrest in Birmingham for having disobeyed an Alabama circuit court order that banned him and other civil rights leaders from taking part in or encouraging demonstrations on the streets of the city.

This plea from the white clergy leaders was the inspiration for King's famous twenty-page response, "Letter from Birmingham Jail," which began as notes on the margins of the *News* and was finished and sent to the press on April 16. Although King recognized in his letter that the clergy had recently demonstrated sympathy for his crusade, he also believed that they had never displayed true morality through all the years that black Birmingham activists were being bombed, stalked, and arrested. He expressed strong disappointment with the "white moderate" who was more devoted to "order" than to justice. The letter explained to the churchmen why blacks could not wait any longer, for "justice too long delayed is justice denied." King wished that the clergy had chosen not to commend the Birmingham police for their "professional discipline," and had commended instead "the Negro sit-inners and demonstrators . . . for their sublime courage, their willingness to suffer and their amazing discipline."[52]

After reading the text of King's lengthy reply, Episcopal Bishop Carpenter remarked to his coadjutor George Murray: "This is what you get when you try to do something. . . . You get it from both sides."[53] Methodist Bishop Harmon was surprised to see King's *Letter from Birmingham Jail* in the newspapers and was deeply disturbed that the civil rights leader was "practically brushing away all we had said."[54] After reading the text, Harmon telephoned his counterpart in the Alabama-West Florida Conference, Paul Hardin, to tell him that King's words were unfair, unjust, and had betrayed himself and all of their fellow clergy.[55] Hardin counseled Harmon not to respond to the document, but the latter continued to be disturbed at what he saw as a "propaganda" press maneuver on King's part. Harmon believed Rabbi Grafman who told him that the letter had actually been written in New York and that King had used the occasion as "a good sounding board to play it on."[56] Harmon held his silence on the letter publicly until later that summer when he was "astonished" to learn that the Methodist Church's National Board of Christian Social Concerns had distributed the King letter along with the names of the Birmingham clergymen appended in an official packet at the conference they held in Chicago.[57] Harmon himself had chosen not to go to Chicago because of a scheduling conflict that August, but he quickly phoned a protest to the delegates that the letter's distribution without consultation was a personal affront.

Harmon later contended that how the King letter was distributed made him and Hardin appear to be "obstacles to all justice and freedom."[58] From Harmon's point of view, the clergy's letter to King was "an attempt to avert the calamities that did happen" (referring to the subsequent confrontations in May between the Birmingham police and young demonstrators).[59] He thought that the Social Concerns gathering did not understand the situation in Birmingham where, in his opinion, a hard core of segregationists had been made more militant by the demonstrations and moderates were becoming greatly embittered by the unrest. There were, Harmon assured the delegates, "unpublicized Negro and white leaders" who were "quietly working with church and civic authorities in many places." In response, the Chicago conference leaders defended their distribution of the letter because they thought that King had eloquently expressed "the complexion of contemporary human relations."[60] Harmon later reflected in his memoirs that King's reply to the ministers helped to make the black leader famous throughout the nation but "did not help us in Birmingham." When in the 1970s, a reporter asked Harmon if he had known Martin Luther King Jr. personally, Harmon replied, "No, all he ever did was just write me a letter."[61]

The Alabama Council on Human Relations, formerly Bob Hughes's biracial organization, was unwilling to alter what clearly had become a matter of highest priority for the Methodists at the national level. The events of the summer of 1963 in Birmingham were doubtless in the delegates' minds when the ACHR went on record in their annual meeting that September calling for the denomination to eliminate the Central Jurisdiction by 1968 and to use church finances to further desegregation. The delegates recommended further that church membership be *clearly available* to anyone regardless of race, that churches be prepared for assignment of pastors without regard for race," and that all of the church's schools, hospitals, homes and agencies should be operated "without racial lines" in employees and members.[62]

For most Alabama Methodists, ACHR's call for full integration came at the end of a summer in which scenes of Birmingham police brutality against nonviolent protestors had been displayed on the front pages of newspapers and magazines throughout the world. In June the North Alabama Conference session had passed a resolution calling for "more peaceful race relations" between whites and blacks in Birmingham.[63] To this end, the NAC representatives on the local Board of Social Concerns, headed by the Reverend Bert Goodwin, called for the conference to institute programs in local churches to lead toward "a more positive plan for Christian action" in improving relations between blacks and whites. During August 1963 the *Alabama Christian Advocate*, after a year of virtual silence on local civil rights issues, printed on its front page an address by Florida Governor LeRoy Collins to the Florida Conference in which he strongly urged the Southern wing of the Methodist Church to speak out against racial bigotry and acts of discrimination. Collins, a prominent Episcopalian layperson, called on Methodists not to take the easy way out by avoiding controversy. "You must be at the outposts," he told his audience, "your ministers are committed to be there, your laymen must back them."[64]

The *Advocate* printed an even more powerful message in early September. Charles Butler, a Methodist missionary who had recently returned to Alabama after two years' service in Panama, exhorted Alabama Methodists to come to terms with the racial questions that presently confronted Christians. "We have sought to narrow the Holy Spirit to certain defined areas of activity," Butler wrote. He saw a "tragic contradiction" between the African mission field, where segregation had never been practiced, and the Methodist Church in the South, where racial barriers had remained in place. "How many of us would receive into our Christian fellowship at home," he wrote, "a Negro who has become Christian through our mission endeavor abroad?"[65] Butler's commentary echoed what a Central Alabama Conference pastor had told Bob Hughes a few years earlier. The minister, quoted anonymously in the ACHR newsletter, assured Hughes that even if all the barriers came down, "Negro Methodists wouldn't rush into your churches—perhaps once in a while someone might visit out of curiosity, but they wouldn't return if they didn't feel welcome."[66]

Only twelve days after this article appeared in the *Advocate*, a cataclysmic event shook to the core many of the "moderate" Methodists whom Butler was addressing: Unknown assailants bombed the black Sixteenth Street Baptist Church on Sunday morning, September 15, killing four black girls just leaving their Sunday school class. An outpouring of grief and outrage came from both blacks and whites. On Wednesday, September 18, among the mourners at a funeral presided over by Martin Luther King Jr. were eight hundred Birmingham pastors of both races.[67]

This one tragedy in 1963, more than any other event, finally moved a number of Methodist ministers in north Alabama to speak out against the old order of segregation. Joe Elmore vividly remembered that Sunday morning when one of his ushers handed him a note giving him news of the explosion.[68] Elmore regarded the Sixteenth Street bombing as the "defining moment" of his ministerial career on the issue of race.[69] The next day he mailed a letter to his Mountain Chapel congregation telling them that he must share some of the blame for what happened that Sunday morning. As a Christian minister, Elmore admitted, he had "often been silent when I should have witnessed to the brotherhood of all."[70] The bombing was for

*Bishop Nolan Harmon*

him an "extreme expression" of some of the attitudes held by a community of which he was a part. The week after the bombing, Elmore attempted to call on the minister of the all-black St. Paul Methodist Church down the block from the Sixteenth Street church. The pastor, the Reverend Dr. Joseph Lowery, was not in, and Elmore's inability to make contact only intensified what Elmore recalled as his "internalized guilt and shame."[71]

The *Alabama Christian Advocate* used these very words at the end of the month in a strained commentary on the bombings. The article noted a more alert and determined attitude among Birmingham's civic and religious leaders to achieve "a harmonious solution to our problems." The writer admitted a "sense of shame and humiliation" over the bombing, and a feeling of "impatience with the law enforcement officials of Birmingham" who had long delayed making arrests for "this and so many other bombings." The options of the past "disappeared in 1954," he admitted, and "mature citizens" must make up their minds to live within the newer court ruling rather than that of "separate but equal."[72] Unlike Elmore, the *Advocate* editorialist chose not to address the lackluster performance of the white Alabama conferences in the intervening years from 1954 to 1963. It had taken almost a full decade for the North Alabama Conference to go on record condemning segregation, and it did so only in the wake of a despicable bombing that served as a wake-up call to the clergy. What the Methodist establishment then faced in north Alabama was not only immediate pressure from the General Conference to remove all racial barriers but also the much more troublesome issue raised by Elmore and a few other ministers: What responsibility must the church bear for the violence and repression that had held a segregated social order in place long after the system no longer had the sanctity and force of national law?

For his part, Bishop Harmon washed his hands of the matter as he left Alabama to return to his full-time duties in the Western North Carolina Conference. A few months later, he abandoned the episcopacy altogether and devoted the next ten years of his life to editing *The Encyclopedia of World Methodism*, a task much more congenial to his temperament. Until his death at the age of one hundred, he defended his conviction that racial integration could only come very gradually to his church and his region. In his memoirs, Harmon recalled making courageous statements against extreme racism during his Alabama tenure, including a speech he made to the North Alabama Conference in which he protested Governor George Wallace's 1963 "Stand in the Schoolhouse Door"—a failed attempt to stop integration at the University of Alabama.[73] He was struck by the fact that he was applauded for his address by integrationists but also received hate letters and "heated rejoinders" from segregationists in his conference.

The bishop began to see that a middle-of-the-road position was not going to solve the church's problems over race in Alabama, but he was unable to find an alternative strategy—just as Elmore had predicted when he heard the bishop speak to the NAC on the subject of the freedom riders in 1961. Duncan Hunter, who was Huntsville's district superintendent during Harmon's episcopacy and knew him well, thought that the bishop was certainly not an overt racist; rather, he was a person who displayed a "kind and loving gentleness" during the three years he served in north Alabama.[74] Harmon's dilemma was that he did not want the Methodist Church in Alabama involved in public issues at a time in its history when it seemed to be lagging far behind the national church.

Taken as a whole, the years from 1960 to 1963 were tumultuous for Alabama Methodists, and particularly for those in the North Alabama Conference. One obvious pattern had emerged concerning progress toward accommodation with the mandates of the national church: those who tended to challenge the system and were open to racial merger were mainly located at relatively unimportant churches in the conference and were mostly younger clergy just beginning their ministries, such as Elmore, Hughes, and Reeves. The two notable exceptions to this were located successively at Birmingham First Methodist. Both Paul Hardin in the 1950s and Denson Franklin in the 1960s were acutely aware of the racial tensions that crystallized into demonstrations only a few blocks from the sanctuary's location on Nineteenth Street North, while other churches located in Birmingham's suburbs or on the fringes formed the phalanx of support for maintaining segregation. Although Highlands Methodist was located on the south side of the city proper, the dynamic leadership of Guy McGowan made it a focal point for organizing the Methodist Layman's Union. Black leaders in the Central Alabama Conference were not participants in NAC discussions concerning merger in this period. In fact, there seemed to be a lack of familiarity with the CAC churches by even the integrationist white ministers.

The most striking events in Alabama Methodism prior to 1964 involved the effective organization of the anti-integrationist forces in the denomination. How to explain this phenomenon? One important factor would be the segregationist leadership in the state, particularly in the Montgomery church headed by G. Stanley Frazer. But the depth of resistance to change is also indicated by the enormous outpouring of support from Methodist laity for the organization of the Methodist Layman's Union. The MLU, like the White Citizens' Councils, could not only boast of business and professional leaders within its ranks, but of judges and lawyers determined to uphold legal segregation. These men had money, social positions, and impressive political power within and without the church. In the face of this extraordinary lay opposition to change, ministers were very reluctant to move in the opposite direction, whatever their personal or spiritual views on integration.

Changes in structure would require changes in leadership at the bishopric level; yet in the decade after the *Brown* decision, two cautious men headed the Methodist Church in Alabama. Bishops Hodge and Harmon were products of the small-town Deep South and had attended seminary at a time when the incompatibility of racial separation with Christian principles was not a topic of debate in their theological studies.

Hodge suffered from poor health throughout his tenure and really wanted to avoid open conflict over any issue. His approach to John Rutland's activities at the Woodlawn church and Bob Hughes's activism with the ACHR was to sidestep any support or identification of his office with them. He was greatly relieved to see Hughes move into the mission field in Africa.

Harmon's reaction to the King letter reveals him to have been perhaps the most conservative of the eight white ministers who requested King to delay his Birmingham demonstrations in 1963. Looking back in his memoirs, Harmon could find little positive to say on his Alabama tenure.

Hodge and Harmon were well-meaning men and not out-and-out racists, but they employed delaying tactics on merger and largely underestimated the significance of the events that placed Birmingham in the center of the civil rights struggle in 1963. The implications of the national and international publicity, given the segregationist system in Alabama were not lost, however, on Methodist leadership at the national level. The Sixteenth Street bombing in mid-September 1963 accelerated pressure within the national church to eliminate racially distinct conferences from the Methodist Church. In Alabama, however, white resistance would remain strong.

## Notes

1. The other Methodist colleges in Alabama were Huntingdon College in Montgomery and Athens College in Athens.

2. Tuell, *Organization,* 120, 121. The lay delegates elected their own representatives to the General Conference and the ministerial delegates did likewise.

3. *Alabama Christian Advocate*, September 22, 1959.

4. *Birmingham News*, September 12, 1959.

5. Hodge to Frank Dominick, April 8, 1959, NACA 6.3, Bishops' Papers.

6. See page 32 for explanation of the "Commission of Seventy" and its hearings throughout the nation in 1957.

7. *Journal of the 1960 General Conference of the Methodist Church* (Nashville: The Methodist Publishing House, 1960), p. 1676.

8. Quoted in Juan Williams, *Eyes on the Prize: America's Civil Rights Years, 1954–1965* (New York: Penguin Books, 1988), 179. Taylor Branch's *Parting the Waters* (cited above) is one of the most authoritative accounts of the interaction between King's Southern Christian Leadership Conference, local Birmingham blacks, and the John F. Kennedy administration.

9. Harrison Salisbury, "Fear and Hatred Grip Birmingham," *New York Times*, April 12, 1960.

10. Charles Morgan, *A Time to Speak* (New York: Harper and Row, 1964), 68.

11. Southern Regional Council Papers (hereinafter SRCP), Lynn-Hendley Research Library (hereinafter LHRL), Birmingham Public Library, Birmingham, Alabama.

12. Morgan, *A Time to Speak,* 71.

13. Hughes to George S. Mitchell, December 20, 1954, SRCP in LHRL.

14. *Alabama Council Newsletter*, April 1959, SRCP in LHRL.

15. Anonymously quoted in *ACHR* Newsletter, May 1959.

16. Undated manuscript, Ed Montgomery Papers, NACA 74.

17. Morgan, *A Time to Speak,* 71.

18. Ibid., 73.

19. Memo, n.d., SRCP in LHRL.

20. Ibid., 73,

21. Vann interview tape, n.d., Robinson. NACA.

22. Morgan, *A Time to Speak,* 73.

23. Rutland interview by Nicholas, February 22, 1996.

24. Undated transcript of interview in Bob Hughes to Ray Goodwin, December 17, 1992, NACA.

25. Morgan, *A Time to Speak,* 83. The Council on Ministries made recommendations to the bishop on the appointment of ministers to their churches and to standing committees of the conference.

26. Quoted in Morgan, *A Time to Speak,* 85.

27. Ibid., 71. Hughes's appointment developed very quickly in September 1960 during the North Alabama Annual Conference meeting as a means of preserving Hughes' ministerial status. Hughes's stay in Rhodesia lasted from January 1961 until July 1964, when both he and Bishop Dodge were declared "prohibited immigrants" and forced to leave. No reason was given but they had constantly opposed the racial policies of the white-controlled government (Randall Jimerson to William Nicholas, February 1, 2015).

28. Bass, *Blessed Are the Peacemakers*, 42.

29. Nolan B. Harmon, *Ninety Years and Counting* (Nashville: Upper Room, 1983), 255.

30. Joseph Mitchell, *There is an Election: Episcopal Elections in the Southeastern Jurisdiction of the United Methodist Church* (Troy, Alabama: Leader Press, 1980), 44.

31. Davis interview tape, May 9, 2001, Robinson, NACA.

32. Quoted in Ed Montgomery interview, February 18, 2002, Nicholas.

33. Duncan Hunter interview tape, April 25, 2001, Robinson, NACA.

34. Bass, *Blessed Are the Peacemakers,* 39.

35. Harmon, *Ninety Years,* 296.

36. *Alabama Christian Advocate*, July 4, 1961.

37. Branch, *Parting the Waters,* 420–421.

38. While the Trailways bus headed toward Birmingham, a second bus carrying freedom

riders was attacked by an angry mob in Anniston, Alabama, and firebombed on its way out of town. The two episodes of local violence against the riders brought the attention of the Kennedy administration to the volatile situation in Alabama, and Kennedy and his brother Attorney General Robert Kennedy attempted unsuccessfully to persuade the segregationist governor of the state, John Patterson, to intervene with local authorities to protect the right of protestors to use interstate transportation. The full story of the freedom riders' episode is told in Raymond Arsenault's *Freedom Riders: 1961 and the Struggle for Racial Justice* (New York: Oxford University Press, 2006).

39. Williams, *Eyes*, 148–149.

40. *Alabama Christian Advocate*, June 6, 1961.

41. *Birmingham News*, May 31, 1961; Elmore interview tape, April 6, 2001, Robinson, NACA.

42. Bass, *Blessed Are the Peacemakers*, 66.

43. Denson Franklin interview, April 30, 1996, Nicholas.

44. Ibid.

45. For the role of Rabbi Grafman in civil rights, see Mark K. Bauman and Berkeley Kalin (eds.), *Quiet Voices: Southern Rabbis and Black Civil Rights, 1880s to 1960s, Judaic Studies Series* (Tuscaloosa: University of Alabama Press, 1997).

46. Branch, *Parting the Waters*, 643.

47. This episode and its relation to the ensuing demonstrations in Birmingham is exhaustively treated by Thornton in *Dividing Lines*. Particularly interesting is Thornton's examination of the Birmingham business community and its realization that the economic future of their retail establishments under the segregation system was in jeopardy. The attack on the freedom riders in Birmingham played a major role in the shift of Sidney Smyer, president of the Chamber of Commerce, from stalwart segregationist with a close relationship with Bull Connor to a position where he realized that the economic future of Birmingham was compromised by Connor's rigidity and coziness with a violent KKK local faction. Smyer's transition is also charted in the comprehensive study by his younger cousin, Diane McWhorter, in her *Carry Me Home: Birmingham, Alabama: The Climactic Battle of the Civil Rights Revolution* (New York: Simon and Schuster, 2001).

48. Williams, *Eyes*, 183.

49. Harmon, *Ninety Years*, 297–298.

50. Bass, *Blessed Are the Peacemakers*, 25.

51. *Birmingham News*, April 13, 1963.

52. King, Martin Luther, Jr., *Why We Can't Wait* (New York, Penguin Books, 1964), 91, 81.

53. Quoted in Branch, *Parting*, 745.

54. Harmon, *Ninety Years*, 229.

55. Bass, *Blessed Are the Peacemakers*, 163.

56. Harmon, *Ninety Years*, 249.

57. *Alabama Christian Advocate*, September 3, 1963.

58. Harmon, *Ninety Years*, 249.

59. *Alabama Christian Advocate*, September 3, 1963.

60. Quoted in Bass, *Blessed Are the Peacemakers*, 106.

61. *Birmingham News*, April 2, 1972.

62. *Alabama Christian Advocate*, September 17, 1963.

63. Ibid., June 25, 1963.

64. Ibid., August 6, 1963.

65. Ibid., September 3, 1963.

66. ACHR *Newsletter*, April, 1959, SRCP in LHRL.

67. Branch, *Parting*, 892.

68. Elmore interview tape, April 6, 2001, Robinson, NACA.

69. Elmore interview, March 1, 1996, Nicholas.

70. Elmore, "Crossings: A Personal Journey Toward Grace," Undated manuscript in possession of author, NACA.

71. Joseph Lowery, who declined to be interviewed for this study, published a collection of his sermons in 2011, but they contain almost no commentary of his pastoral years in the Central and then North Alabama Conference. See Joseph Lowery, *Singing the Lord's Song in a Foreign Land* (Nashville: Abingdon Press, 2011).

72. *Alabama Christian Advocate*, October 1, 1963.

73. Harmon, *Ninety Years*. 297.

74. Hunter interview tape, April 25, 2001, Robinson, NACA.

# III.

# Kenneth Goodson Comes to Alabama, 1964–1966

By the time of the quadrennial General Conference of the Methodist Church in April 1964 in Pittsburgh, Pennsylvania, the impetus for ending segregation in the South had shifted somewhat from protests and demonstrations in the South to comprehensive action by the federal government. This change began with the ascension of Vice President Lyndon B. Johnson to the presidency following the assassination of President John F. Kennedy in November 1963. Kennedy had only gradually come to support civil rights legislation after he witnessed the violence against demonstrators in Birmingham and other Deep South cities. Kennedy's hopes that black and white Southerners would agree to a gradual desegregation were replaced by a realization that as African American demands for full citizenship increased, white Southern support for segregation remained entrenched, and thus there likely could be no peaceful compromise. In the early summer of 1963, Kennedy proposed a sweeping civil rights bill that would desegregate all public accommodations and protect the voting rights of African Americans. His speech was followed in August 1963 by the "March for Jobs and Freedom," attended by an estimated 250,000 persons—black and white—who had trekked to Washington, D.C., from across the nation. It was at this rally that Martin Luther King Jr., standing on the steps of the Lincoln Memorial, delivered his historic "I have a Dream" speech calling for an end to racism.

Unfortunately, white Southerners in Congress managed to bottle up the civil rights bill in a House committee, and Kennedy was unable to muster enough votes to move it forward before he was killed. The new president, however, made the civil rights bill a priority during his first month in office. In his first address to a joint session of Congress, Johnson told the legislators that passage of a civil rights bill would be a lasting memorial to Kennedy's memory. Over the next few months, Johnson's masterful leadership and knowledge of the machinery of Congress resulted in the bill's release from committee and the beginning of a debate in the Senate in which the President's allies defeated a filibuster and brought the bill finally to a successful vote by both houses of Congress in July 1964.

As Peter Murray has pointed out in his study of the Methodist Church and race, there was a convergence of events in American society and the Methodist church in the early 1960s. Civil rights had become such a powerful issue that the nation's political establishment could not ignore it. Methodist leaders discovered, the Kennedy administration had, that even concrete solutions for change did not insure progress from recalcitrant segregationists. There would be no easy solutions to the church's problem of racial division.[1] A shift in attitudes in the Methodist Church could be seen at the Methodist Human Relations Conference in 1963, the one which distributed copies of King's "Letter from Birmingham Jail" to the disgust of Bishop Harmon. At that Chicago conference, more than eleven hundred Methodists discussed race relations and recommended that the timetable to abolish the Central Jurisdiction be shortened. Furthermore, they stated that nondiscrimination should be a policy for all Methodist-related facilities, including schools, hospitals, orphanages, and retirement homes.

The 1964 General Conference marked the emergence of Presiding Bishop Gerald Kennedy as an effective advocate of a desegregated church structure. Kennedy was a relatively young bishop at fifty-two, and his photo had appeared on the cover of *Time* magazine.[2] His opening address revealed him to be a powerful orator. He told the delegates that segregation within the church could no longer be justified on the basis of "weird interpretations of the Scriptures. . . . Prejudice against any person because of color or social status is a sin." "Every district superintendent," the bishop continued, would be "bound by the discipline of the Church" to oppose segregation and discrimination.[3] His speech came close to proclaiming that racial merger was now compulsory.

Following Kennedy's lead, the newly formed Commission on Social Concerns presented a report recommending a plan to abolish the black

Central Jurisdiction by the end of 1968. The plan proposed full integration in three stages: First the black annual conferences comprising the Central Jurisdiction would be realigned to fall into the boundaries of the white conferences. Then the Central Jurisdiction conferences would be transferred into the white jurisdictions by a series of referendums held in each annual conference. Within each jurisdiction final merger would take place with black churches participating fully within the administrative structure of the formerly all-white conferences.[4] The ensuing discussion was dominated by those who believed that the 1939 structure had become an embarrassment with the Central Jurisdiction representing a symbol of segregation within Methodism. The report's three-part mechanism did offer an olive branch to the white Southern delegates if they would view the process as preserving the principle of constitutional voluntarism. But they instead saw in the plan a violation of the promise offered in 1956 by the old Amendment IX, which would have given the white Southern conferences a voice in the final conference structure. In the end, the General Conference approved the 1968 plan nearly unanimously; there were only twelve dissenting votes. The outcome of the so-called "voluntary" process was evident from the outset: the elimination of the Central Jurisdiction.

Back in Alabama, the new merger plan again divided the clergy and the laity along generational lines. The senior lay leadership at Canterbury Methodist Church, in the affluent and virtually all-white Birmingham suburb of Mountain Brook, sent a petition to the General Conference in which they proposed a states' rights approach. Sidney Smyer, active in the Methodist Layman's Union and secretary of the Canterbury board of stewards, wrote that neither the local conference nor the national church should "attempt to impose views, procedures or doctrines" on each other. With no mention of the General Conference's pronouncements on racial separation, the board emphasized Southerners' "marvelous homogeneity and civilization" and presented themselves as a "proud people" who would deny the "ravages of change."[5] The *Alabama Christian Advocate* spoke out in an editorial that warned national church officials against "forced progress" on the proposed merger deadline of 1968 and took exception to the "coercion" they found in Bishop Kennedy's remarks.[6]

In contrast, ministers who were sympathetic and supportive of merger saw an opportunity to move the North Alabama Conference forward at the annual meeting in Birmingham in June 1964. A member of the conference Board of Christian Social Concerns, Emory Burton, proposed in a late Thursday afternoon session that the Central Alabama Conference be invited to send delegates as observers to the North Alabama Conference at its next meeting.[7] Supporters of the surprise resolution were present in sufficient numbers to pass the proposal on a voice vote and probably caught the delegates at a time when many had already gone home for the day. The next morning the Birmingham district superintendent, R. E. Kimbrough, engineered a successful reconsideration of the resolution, and the matter was referred back to the Board of Social Concerns for further study—thus quashing the possibility for an inclusive meeting in 1965.[8] Apparently a press report on Friday morning that the Methodists were moving toward integration had played a role in the withdrawal of the motion, but, more significantly, the episode was a sign that younger ministers in the conference were now willing to take a more aggressive stand on merger. In its first report in 1961, the local Board of Christian Social Concerns had stated that Christianity required a concern for the freedom of all; and the next year the report recommended, in the words of Joe Elmore, that the conference "examine our own lives and attitudes and seek communication across racial lines."[9] The more conservative and older clergy were anxious to slow down the process. Bishop Harmon's own view was that the matter should never have been raised on the conference floor but was more properly left up to the presiding bishop—in other words, himself.[10]

By the end of the 1964 sessions, many of the younger NAC clergy were frustrated on the issue of compliance with the Pittsburgh plan of integration. Lay leaders who had supported the invitation to the Central Alabama Conference were also restive and resentful of conference leadership. As Ross A. Sheldon, chair of the Division of Human Relations and Economic Affairs, wrote to his committee members, it was the "young tigers" who rose to do battle on the floor of the conference, and the "bald-headed row" either sat quietly or spoke for a "don't rock the boat" point of view. "It would help," continued Sheldon, if the "older, better known and acknowledged leaders" of the conference would speak on behalf of the upcoming reforms in conference structure.[11] The younger church leaders clearly wanted more aggressive leadership from the top on the issue and were deeply disappointed in Bishop Harmon's policy of avoidance.

Outside Alabama, however, changes in church leadership were underway. The Southeastern Jurisdiction elected four new bishops in 1964, and the first of these, W. Kenneth Goodson, was assigned to succeed Nolan Harmon in leading the North Alabama Conference and Paul Hardin in the Alabama-West Florida Conference. Goodson had been a district superintendent and a pastor of several large churches in North Carolina. On the surface, there was little to suggest that Goodson was very different from most Southern-born bishops. His family background was modest. One of eight children of a railroad engineer, Goodson retained from his childhood loves of passenger trains and traditional Methodist hymns.[12]

Following graduation from Duke Divinity School in the class of 1937, Goodson's reputation as a forceful and effective preacher had paved his way to important posts.[13] He exhibited a strong sense of humor and a remarkable ability to remember names. Unlike Nolan Harmon, Goodson was not a scholar and never distinguished himself in writing for publication. He apparently deliberately chose the Deep South as his preferred appointment.[14] In the two white Alabama conferences, Goodson found a post that had about 200,000 members, three colleges, a children's home, and a summer camp at Sumatanga. At the time of his election to the episcopacy, Goodson was regarded by his peers as fairly conservative on racial issues; he had sought to defeat a motion at the 1964 General Conference which he found condescending to the South.[15]

Goodson was only fifty-one when appointed in August 1964, and his physical and mental energy contrasted with Alabama's two previous bishops. More importantly, whereas Harmon had stayed in a Birmingham hotel while his family remained in North Carolina, the Goodson family would make their home in Birmingham. Shortly after his election, the new bishop visited Birmingham with his wife and then sent a letter to all the clergy informing them that his office would always be open to them.[16] By early September 1964, the Goodsons were living in Birmingham, and he involved himself very quickly and energetically in the life of his two conferences.

The new bishop's approach to his job was certain to make him a popular and effective church leader. Not content to stay in his office, he began to undertake a crowded schedule of Sunday morning sermons, dedications of new church buildings, and stewardship campaigns throughout the state. In contrast to his bookish predecessor, Goodson was very personable. One of the younger ministers at that time recalled that he "awed the laity. . . . They fell in love with him."[17] Another observer remembered that Goodson was "articulate, humorous and very forthright."[18] Many Alabama Methodists came to regard Goodson as a personal friend, and he obviously had the ability to make them believe that their story or situation was of vital personal interest to him.

Goodson was aware of the newly emerging importance of electronic media coverage for the Methodist Church and began a series of weekly half-hour radio programs. Carried on about twenty stations, "The Bishop's Hour" featured short sermons by Goodson and special music by a choir made up of ministers from the two conferences.[19] This program proved so popular that it was later expanded to a television format. Everett Holley, who was program director at Birmingham's Channel Thirteen (WVTM), recalled that the dynamic Goodson controlled every aspect of the program as if he owned the station.[20] Goodson also wrote a "Bishop's Corner" column in the *Alabama Christian Advocate* that became one of its most popular features. The weekly column gave the impression of a bishop who was constantly on the move throughout the entire state. Goodson unfailingly had good things to say about his ministers, their wives and families, and the good food served at their tables after the Sunday service. His writing style was expansive and folksy; he almost never assumed the attitude of piety or sternness often displayed by former bishops in their *Advocate* writings. His columns read like a travelogue of backcountry Alabama, with Goodson admitting that his secretary or wife often drove the car while he prepared his column for next week's edition.

Goodson developed the practice of answering personally—with grace and wit—each letter he received, no matter how critical. His letters made for lively reading. When the *Birmingham News* reported that a local minister and his wife appeared on the Johnny Carson NBC television show and sang a song about "beer and pretzels," Goodson responded to a query by writing that the song was not "the kind of music I am personally attracted to, but . . . I think we have to give each other a degree of freedom in our expressions."[21] At the same time, his letters displayed tactful honesty and sometimes exasperation. To a steward at Birmingham First Methodist who wrote the bishop complaining about a newspaper report that a North Carolina conference had given one million dollars to Martin Luther King's crusade, Goodson wrote that "someday I'm going to get all you Methodists together and whip the whole lot of you. You believe anything anybody tells you and you take it as Gospel." As a North Carolina native, Goodson could assure the writer that the conference in question "had never appropriated $1,000,000 for anything, either sin or salvation."[22]

Goodson established his presence in Alabama churches by accepting invitations to give sermons throughout the state. His vibrant personality was felt most forcibly in these homilies. He was a North Carolina storyteller in the best Southern tradition and effectively interjected humor into his sermons and speeches. Goodson excelled in the art of personal self-disclosure, peppering his messages with real-life episodes from his experiences in the church. He was fond of reading letters received from his conferences. By the time Goodson arrived in Alabama, he had developed a style of speaking that displayed certain vocal characteristics: he would bear down on the letter "G" to emphasize such words as "glory" or God," employed King James English with its use of "thee" and "thou," and used such archaic expressions such as "yea" and "verily." His style in his sermons was florid. One observer remembered a typical sentence might be, "we have come to talk about some things that we ought to talk about and to remember some things that we ought to remember and to resolve never to forget some things we ought never to forget."[23] Goodson had no doubt of his ability and power to mesmerize an audience. Once after his fellow bishop and friend Paul Hardin bested him on the golf course and bragged about it, Goodson retorted, "But don't you wish you could preach like me."[24] Another bishop in Virginia recalled, "To hear him speak or preach was always an event. And we didn't want to preach anytime soon . . . where he had just held forth.[25]

*Bishop Kenneth Goodson on the set of his television show on Birmingham's WAPI-TV, channel 13, in the mid-1960s.*

The new bishop's first half year of service in Alabama did not emphasize a subject which must have been much on his mind and those of his listeners as well: the racial turmoil in the state. Goodson was certainly aware when he accepted his two bishoprics that he was going to a state in the midst of a racial crisis. He often remarked on the fact that as the Methodist bishop in Alabama, he had within his flock Governor George C. Wallace, Bull Connor, and an Alabama KKK leader, Bobby Shelton.[26] The expectations of John Rutland and other clergy were that Goodson would provide vigorous leadership in race relations. Rutland wrote within a month of Goodson's arrival asking that he speak out on the importance of "racial brotherhood" in keeping with the programs of the Methodist Church.[27] Given the prominence of the White Citizens' Councils and the recent activities of the Methodist Layman's Union, Rutland thought that Goodson needed to preach about the "sin of racism."

Rutland and his colleagues were not initially impressed. They believed Goodson to be an ambitious man who had wanted very much to be a bishop. Rutland recalled that Goodson name-dropped (boasting about a conversation with his "best friend," Jack Kennedy) and that his theology consisted of a traditional plank of "anti-gambling, anti-alcohol and prayer."[28] Duncan Hunter, district superintendent in Huntsville and a minister many regarded as the conference intellectual, also considered Goodson to be an ambitious bishop, and unprepared for the level of racism he encountered in Alabama. Having come from the more open environment of Duke University, Goodson did not immediately realize the deep divisions in the North Alabama Conference over the issue of merger. He believed, according to Hunter, that he could "settle differences over dinner" in a Birmingham club or restaurant.[29] Likewise, Louise Branscomb, a Birmingham gynecologist and prominent leader among Methodist women in Alabama, at first thought Goodson to be "an affable person" who wouldn't "stand up for his convictions too strongly."[30]

Some clergy, however, suspected that Goodson was simply being circumspect on the racial issue and, as Denson Franklin put it, "feeling his way at first."[31] Joe Elmore believed that Goodson knew full well what coming to Birmingham meant in terms of the "strong witness" he would have to offer on the race question.[32] Bill Davis, who would become one of Goodson's district superintendents, thought that Goodson was well aware of what was expected of him on the racial question: Goodson was "like a man under orders, conscience bound to bring [merger] to pass. It was the key issue and concern of all his administration."[33]

Perhaps Goodson's personal charm obscured views on merger and race that he had held for a long time. A black Methodist minister recalled much later that while he had been a shoeshine boy at a High Point, North Carolina, hotel, Goodson's treating him "like I was somebody" had inspired him to go into the ministry.[34] Perhaps many integrationists in Alabama Methodism were inclined to underestimate Goodson's effectiveness because the bishop relied so much on his winning personality. As Bert Goodwin remembered, Goodson was the "perfect politician who knew how to employ people to get things done: a dinner here and there, a golf date here and there."[35] This

*Reverend John Rutland*

was Goodson's way: to be deliberate in moving his conferences toward racial inclusiveness.

Early in his episcopacy, Goodson began to develop a personal relationship with the younger generation of clergy. His first contact might take the form of using them as chauffeurs to drive him around the state as he made his frequent forays into small Alabama towns. Joe Elmore recalled that he came to know Goodson well as he drove him from one speaking engagement to another.[36] What Elmore did not realize was that Goodson was assessing his leadership capabilities. Similarly, a young Robert C. ("Bob") Morgan came to the attention of Goodson through the personal recommendations of Duncan Hunter and John Rutland. Goodson visited Huntsville's Epworth Church, where Morgan was pastor, to preach in the new sanctuary, and he was impressed with the growth of the membership under Morgan's leadership.[37] Morgan was the first of the younger clergy whom Goodson elevated to a district superintendent position (Morgan eventually became a bishop), followed by Barry Anderson (1967) and Elmore (1968), both under age forty.

Although some grumbled behind the scenes about the appointment of these junior clergy, Goodson's appointment-making powers were virtually unlimited as a bishop, and he named more than forty new superintendents in both conferences in his eight years in Alabama. Many were in their early thirties or forties.[38] Through his contacts with the young ministers and lay leaders, Goodson became well-acquainted with the divisions within the North Alabama Conference over the merger issue. Communication with Ross Sheldon gave Goodson full knowledge of the turmoil that the conference had experienced the previous year over whether to invite Central Alabama Conference ministers to the annual meeting as observers. Sheldon and his Division of Human Relations and Economic Affairs decided not to reintroduce the resolution on the floor of the 1965 NAC meeting and made the recommendation for inclusion directly to Goodson.[39] By sending his division's support for a "fraternal exchange" of delegates to Goodson for action, Sheldon was hoping that the new bishop would handle the matter behind the scenes. As Sheldon told a fellow member, "I don't think we want a repeat of last year's donnybrook," which would present a conference in turmoil to the press and the public.[40]

Goodson was also beginning to realize the depth of his laity's conservative reaction to many Methodist programs. As he wrote to Duncan Hunter, "the North Alabama Conference had given very little money to the national church's World Service and had defaulted more than 60 percent on pledges to Methodist educational institutions."[41] Ten months after arriving in Alabama, Goodson complained that his desk was cluttered daily with letters saying, "I don't like this and I don't like that, so I won't pay World Service or I'll take out the literature, or a dozen other things. . . ." "Where is the personal loyalty to the church and the Annual Conference," Goodson asked, as "this is Methodist literature; World Service is a Methodist cause." His letters to persons who complained to him about the national church's agenda were diplomatically worded, but he also directly addressed the issues raised in the context of Christian values. In answer to a Republican layman who threatened to withhold contributions from his church because he thought national church literature was opposed to Barry Goldwater's social ideas, Goodson sidestepped a discussion of candidates and partisan politics. "There are social implications of the gospel," he wrote to a critic, "and most of the time I know that its social message comes closer to being right than they do." He concluded, "I believe in a social order [that has] to be based on the teachings of Jesus Christ."[42] Goodson's approach to the conference turmoil and dissension was to put the best face on the situation in public by rarely commenting to the press on such problems. In his contacts with national church officials, the bishop was invariably optimistic about the Alabama conferences. He wrote Presiding Bishop Gerald Kennedy that "we are going to win our battle. . . . Our course is set and we are on the way."[43]

In Selma during March 1965—a fateful time in a fateful place—Goodson's own position on the civil rights movement became clearer. He accepted an invitation to dedicate a new church and address a large group of Methodist laymen in the Selma District on Sunday, March 7. While he was speaking, the events that came to be known as "Bloody Sunday" were unfolding a few blocks away. Following almost a year of black voter voting registration attempts that had met with white resistance, hostility, and violence, an activist had been killed in February in nearby Marion by an Alabama highway patrolman. Martin Luther King Jr., now a Nobel peace prize laureate, had preached the slain man's funeral, and afterwards a protest march was announced from Selma to the state capitol in Montgomery to symbolically lay the blame for Alabama's racial turmoil at the feet of Governor George C. Wallace. On March 7, a column of demonstrators left downtown Selma and paraded peacefully across the Edmund Pettus Bridge on U.S. Highway 80. At the base of the bridge on the Montgomery side of the Alabama River, the marchers' path was blocked by ranks of state patrolmen and a posse of sheriff's deputies, some on horseback. After a brief face-off, the marchers were beaten and tear-gassed by the law enforcement officers. Newspaper photographers and television cameramen recorded the assault for the national media.[44]

When Goodson emerged from the church that he was dedicating, he learned of the events. That evening the bishop fulfilled a speaking engagement in Montgomery and then stayed for a two-day conference with church leaders from the Alabama-West Florida Conference. Before he left Montgomery on Tuesday afternoon, Goodson arranged a meeting with Governor Wallace (a Methodist) that he later described as a "pastoral call." Although the meeting between the governor and the bishop was scheduled to last fifteen minutes, it continued for over an hour. According to Goodson's account in "The Bishop's Corner," he expressed to Wallace his disapproval of the violence that had occurred in Selma.[45] The governor, for his part, expressed "deep regret that the incident had occurred." The rest of the hour was devoted to the topic of "human relations," and Goodson assured his readers that the two had prayed together. Much later, Bishop Harmon provided more details of the meeting based on a conversation he had with Goodson. According to Harmon, Wallace was adamant in his refusal to permit the Selma march but asked Goodson what he should do next. "I would open that bridge," the bishop replied, "You have forces ready for any trouble."[46] Wallace's decision to allow the subsequent opening of the bridge to the protestors may have been influenced by Goodson's advice, but it is more likely that the governor was persuaded by the unfavorable international media attention that the "Bloody Sunday" had brought to his state and by the federal court ordering the state not only to allow the march but to protect it.

Goodson himself was embarrassed by the fact that prominent church officials from his own denomination came to Alabama to participate in the well-publicized march a few days later. King and SCLC had sent telegrams to ministers of all faiths asking them to take part in a symbolic demonstration of support for a new national voting rights law. The National Council of Churches responded by urging its denominational members to heed King's invitation. Goodson quietly appealed to his colleagues in other episcopacies not to participate in the march. Among the Methodists who made the journey to Alabama was Bishop John Wesley Lord from the conference that included Washington, D.C. Goodson believed that Lord was discourteous by not informing the Alabama hierarchy of his plans and that "he could have made a better contribution by staying out."[47] But Goodson also accepted the reality of the situation: the state and the church must "measure up to the demands of this hour," he told his readers in the *Advocate*. He urged Alabama Methodists not only to obey the law, but to play a role in the struggle for reconciliation between the races in future months.

Following the Selma march, Goodson called an unpublicized meeting in Birmingham's Tutwiler Hotel of selected Methodist ministers in the North Alabama Conference. According to Denson Franklin, who was present, the group was highly representative, including all the district superintendents and leaders from both large and small congregations. It was obvious to all assembled that Goodson had been deeply saddened by the events in Selma, and he even wept as he asked the group for their support in drafting what had to be a "strong and firm statement, but one made in love."[48] The outcome of this gathering was an official "pastoral letter" that Goodson requested be read from church pulpits on Sunday, April 4. The bishop knew that his words on behalf of racial relations would be unpopular in some quarters of his church, but this was, he wrote, a chance he had to take.[49] In the letter, Goodson used what was for him the key word on behalf of racial justice: "reconciliation." From his perspective, the Methodist Church in Alabama must admit its part in the sin of racism and become "an instrument of healing the wounds which have been chronic in our society." In this task of reconciliation, Methodists must commit themselves to "the elimination of those injustices that bar any of our people from full participation in all the rights of citizenship." This effort must support, above all, the fair administration of voter requirements for "all of our people."

Goodson's statement was important. A Methodist leader in the Deep South was speaking out against the segregationist order. According to the *Advocate*, Goodson's pastoral letter drew national attention as the "finest utterance on the subject to come out of the South in all the long period of current racial unrest."[50]

Goodson's statement came at a time when the civil rights movement was forcing clergy and laity in Alabama to reassess their personal adherence to segregation within their own congregations. For many Methodists, the question was a difficult one: What should be their response to blacks who might come to their sanctuaries for a Sunday worship service? The Methodist Church's *Discipline* clearly stated that congregations could not "refuse access to worship "on a basis of race, color, national origin, or economic condition."[51] There was no unanimity on this issue in Alabama. In early 1965, Ross Sheldon, still chair of the Division of Human Relations and Economic Affairs, forwarded to Goodson an official statement by the General Board of the Methodist Church that clearly stated the illegality of barring entry to any black worshippers.[52] Sheldon anticipated that "kneel-ins" by civil rights workers would occur in the upcoming summer months. He feared that those churches that blocked the entry of blacks would be open to civil suits and that the most troublesome possibility would be that local law enforcement might be called in—with disastrous results. The *Alabama Christian Advocate* underscored Sheldon's worries later that summer by carrying a strong editorial against the exclusion of any persons who might wish to attend a service in a Methodist church.[53] The *Advocate* cited the latest version of the *Social Creed*, adopted in 1960, that pledged openness to "any person because of race, color, or national origin," and condemned the point of view that churches were "just an exclusive club."[54]

At issue in these confrontations on church steps was the often delicate balance of authority between a pastor and his congregation. Denson Franklin, pastor of the influential Birmingham First Methodist Church, remembered that one Sunday evening about this time, Harry Denman spoke at the evening service; with him were two black friends. One of the most dynamic Methodist lay leaders in the state, Denman was outspoken in his conviction that the church must open its doors to all persons regardless of race. One of Franklin's ushers that night threatened to go into the congregation and take Denman's friends out bodily. "I stopped this immediately," recalled Franklin, "by telling him that I would go down and sit with them if need be."[55] Claude Whitehead at Alexander City First Methodist recollected that some churches hired guards to make sure that blacks did not enter their sanctuaries.[56] Whitehead was grateful when two of his lay leaders came to him and told him that the ushers had agreed to let them handle any situation that might arise with blacks who might come to services. "If they come with a respectful attitude," they told him, "we will see that they are courteously seated. We know that you can't preach if we are turning persons away from worship." Not all ushers were so cooperative. Peggy Mauldin at Hueytown Methodist quoted an usher as telling her, "I will shoot the first Negro who comes in the church."[57]

While individual congregations were confronting the issue of admitting blacks to their services, work was underway on other fronts. At the 1966 conference session, Ross Sheldon's committee proposed a resolution affirming that all Methodist churches were open to worshippers of all races. The assembled delegates weakened the draft statement by substituting a rewording that recognized that individual churches in the conference were "making sincere efforts toward a Christ-like reconciliation in the sensitive area of race relations." The secret ballot on this alternative motion resulted in 315 votes in favor and 229 against. Joe Elmore's observation on the outcome was that the conservatives chose to hide behind some "pious words about praying for each other."[58]

Under Bishop Goodson's authority the North Alabama Conference was moving toward an ad hoc accommodation with the Central Alabama Conference leadership. One of Goodson's closest friends was Harold De Wolf of the Boston University School of Theology, who had taught Martin Luther King Jr. during his seminary education. In the summer of 1965, at De Wolf's urging, Goodson invited the ranking CAC ministers to participate in the Alabama Pastor's School at Blue Lake Camp near Andalusia.[59] Goodson relayed his decision to district superintendents in both his conferences, and his letters to them revealed that he was beginning with what he described as "the least possible thing" by inviting the four black district superintendents to "come in for a day."[60] "I wish we could tell them to come along for the whole school, he wrote, but I guess we had better flavor the soup a little before we serve it in its entirety." To another minister he wrote, "I wish they could stay the whole time, but I guess I won't ask them to stay overnight."[61]

Goodson's inclusion of the black church officials in the summer seminar was done quickly and on the highest leadership level. Meanwhile rank-and-file white ministers in the North Alabama Conference began to reach out to their black colleagues in the Central Alabama Conference. In 1964, Elmore had gone to talk with Charles L. Hutchinson about setting up an encounter group with black ministers in Hutchinson's Birmingham district. After checking with his own district superintendent, Elmore, along with fellow white ministers Bill Miles, Pete Furio, and George Quiggle, set up a meeting with Joseph Lowery and other black ministers at St. Paul Method-ist Church in downtown Birmingham. For the next two years, the group met monthly at the NAC Grace Church in east Birmingham for discussion and an informal worship service. According to Elmore, there had been such total separation of the two clergies that much of the time was devoted to "elementary sharing and building understanding."[62] The whites had to learn how to pronounce Negro correctly, and the blacks had to adjust to the use of the word "preacher" by the white ministers. One black minister told of his anger at a white workman who called him "preacher," a term that often was used in the segregationist past to address any black man who wore a tie."[63] While Goodson did not take part in these Birmingham meetings between his ministers and their black counterparts, he was surely aware that Elmore, Furio, and other young ministers were beginning the process of "reconciliation" that he had stressed in his pastoral letter of the preceding April.

By the NAC's 1966 annual meeting, Goodson had begun to steer Alabama Methodists toward compliance with the national church's mandate for complete merger. In June, the delegates voted 345 to 194 to comply with the General Conference's mandate to allow the Central Alabama Conference to be placed within the boundaries of the white conferences.[64] This meant in practice that the black Alabama churches would be moved into the two white Alabama conferences as a unit. The larger and difficult issue was *when* the all-black jurisdiction would be made completely a part of the majority white administrative units. Ironically, if merger had occurred at this point the percentage of black Methodists in the North Alabama Conference would have constituted a tiny fraction: less than 3 percent of its total membership, and about 3 percent of the Alabama-West Florida Conference ranks.[65]

Within less than two years, Kenneth Goodson had reversed the lethargy of the North Alabama Conference in regard to the racial questions facing the church. His dynamic personality and non-confrontational style endeared him to both sides in the merger debate. He used his considerable power as bishop to bring a younger generation of ministers into positions of authority within his own cabinet, particularly through the appointment of new district superintendents. At the same time, his own perception of the magnitude of racial injustice in the state broadened, and after Selma, Goodson was emotionally and spiritually committed to folding the black membership of the Central Conference into the two white Alabama conferences.

## NOTES

1. Murray, p. 138.
2. Ibid, p. 154.
3. Ibid., May 12, 1964.
4. *Alabama Christian Advocate*, March 31, 1964.
5. Ibid., April 28, 1964.
6. Ibid., June 23, 1964.
7. The Board of Social Concerns was created at the national level by the merger in 1960 of the Board of Temperance, the Board of World Peace and the Board of Social and Economic Relations. Each conference then had a local counterpart to the general agency, and the members were appointed by the bishop of that conference

8.   *Alabama Christian Advocate*, June 23, 1964.

9.   Elmore interview tape, April 6, 2001, Robinson, NACA.

10.   Kenneth Goodson to Ross A. Sheldon, February 16, 1965, NACA 6.2, Bishops' Papers.

11.   Undated memorandum by Sheldon, NACA 6.2, Bishops' Papers.

12.   "W. Kenneth Goodson, "Recollection of Early Years" [Transcript of interview by W. Kenneth Goodson with Alecia Laws], in *Walter Kenneth Goodson: A Life* (Commemorative Edition, *Virginia United Methodist Heritage*, 1993), 6.

13.   Thomas A. Stockton, "W. Kenneth Goodson: The North Carolina Years," in *Walter Kenneth Goodson: A Life* (Commemorative Edition, *Virginia United Methodist Heritage*, 1993), 14–15.

14.   Joseph M. Mitchell, "'We are at Our Best When the Wolves are Howling': Walter Kenneth Goodson's Episcopacy in Alabama-West Florida Methodism, 1964–1972," in *Walter Kenneth Goodson: A Life* (Commemorative Edition, *Virginia United Methodist Heritage*, 1993), 24.

15.   Joseph M. Mitchell, *There is an Election*, 69.

16.   Mitchell, "We Are at Our Best," 26.

17.   Davis interview tape, May 9, 2001, Robinson, NACA.

18.   Ted Leach interview tape, April 15, 2001, Robinson, NACA.

19.   Mitchell, "We Are at Our Best," 31.

20.   Leach interview tape, April 25, 2001, Robinson, NACA.

21.   Goodson to Larry Adcock, May 21, 1969, NACA 6.3, Bishops' Papers.

22.   Goodson to Edward B. Dismukes, August 2, 1964, ibid.

23.   Diedra H. Kriewald, "He Loved to Tell the Story: The Preaching of W. Kenneth Goodson," in *Walter Kenneth Goodson: A Life* (Commemorative Edition, *Virginia United Methodist Heritage*, 1993), 39, 40.

24.   Carter T, Holbrook Jr., "W. Kenneth Goodson: The Pastor," in *Walter Kenneth Goodson: A Life* (Commemorative Edition, *Virginia United Methodist Heritage*, 1993), 22.

25.   L. Bevel Jones, II, "Memoir, Southeastern Jurisdictional Conference," in *Walter Kenneth Goodson: A Life* (Commemorative Edition, *Virginia United Methodist Heritage*, 1993), 3.

26.   Mitchell, "We Are at our Best," 36.

27.   Rutland to Goodson, September 16, 1964, NACA 6.2, Bishops' Papers.

28.   Rutland, *Mary and Me*, 122.

29.   Hunter interview, Nicholas, October 25, 1996, NACA.

30.   Louise Branscom interview, Nicholas, March 19, 1996, NACA.

31.   Denson Franklin interview, Nicholas, April 30, 1996, NACA.

32.   Elmore interview, Nicholas, March 1, 1996, NACA.

33.   Davis interview tape, May 9, 2001, Robinson, NACA.

34.   Holbrook, "Goodson: The Pastor," 19.

35.   Bert Goodwin interview, Nicholas, April 13, 2002, NACA.

36.   Joe Elmore Interview, Nicholas, May 8, 2002, NACA.

37.   Morgan Interview tape, Robinson, May 9, 2001, NACA.

38. Mitchell, "We Are at Our Best," 32–33.

39. Sheldon to Goodson, n.d., NACA 6.2, Bishops' Papers.

40. Ross to B. H. Haynes, November 27, 1964, NACA 6.2, Bishops' Papers.

41. Goodson to Hunter, July 15, 1965, NACA 6.2, Bishops' Papers.

42. Goodson to Kenneth E. Traweek, September 17, 1964, NACA 6.2, Bishops' Papers.

43. Goodson to Kennedy, April 27, 1965, NACA 6.2, Bishops' Papers.

44. The aftermath of the March 7 Selma episode involved much behind-the-scenes maneuvering between King and the Lyndon B. Johnson administration, a federal court ruling asserting the demonstrators' right to march, and the eventual federalization of the Alabama National Guard to protect the continuation of the Selma-to-Montgomery march with King and national clerics and celebrities leading the way. See Thornton's *Dividing Lines*, 413–499, for an authoritative account of local issues in the Selma story, including tensions between the SCLC, SNCC, and the local black community.

45. *Alabama Christian Advocate*, March 16, 1965.

46. Nolan B. Harmon, "Foreword," in *Walter Kenneth Goodson: A Life* (Commemorative Edition, *Virginia United Methodist Heritage*, 1993), 1.

47. *Alabama Christian Advocate*, March 23, 1965.

48. Franklin interview, Nicholas, April 30, 1996, NACA.

49. *Alabama Christian Advocate*, April 6, 1965.

50. Ibid, June 19, 1965.

51. Methodist Church *Discipline* (1964): 106.1 (p. 49).

52. Sheldon to Goodson, March 11, 1965, NACA 6.2, Bishops' Papers

53. *Alabama Christian Advocate*, June 27, 1965.

54. By this time (1965) the General Conference had revised the *Methodist Social Creed* to include a section on human rights, and this was the source for the *Advocate's* editorial. The first statement of the *Social Creed* had appeared in 1908, and had been revised occasionally to reflect a more inclusive viewpoint on social problems. The Creed was supposed to be read from the pulpit once a year, but according to the *Discipline* was not "binding" on individual congregations.

55. Franklin interview, Nicholas, April 30, 1996, NACA.

56. Claude Whitehead, "Memories of Alexander City First Methodist Church, 1962–1967," undated manuscript in possession of author.

57. Peggy Mauldin interview, Nicholas, February 10, 1996, NACA.

58. Elmore interview tape, April 6 2001, Robinson, NACA.

59. De Wolf to Goodson, June 10, 1965, NACA 6.2, Bishops' Papers.

60. Goodson to Don Collins, July 6, 1965, NACA 6.2, Bishops' Papers.

61. Goodson to C. Everett Barnes, July 6, 1965, NACA 6.2, Bishops' Papers.

62. Elmore interview, Nicholas, February 22, 1996, NACA.

63. Elmore, "Crossings."

64. *Alabama Christian Advocate*, June 14, 1966.

65. *Alabama Christian Advocate*, November 1, 1966.

# IV.

# The Battle for Merger, 1966–1972

The years 1965 to 1968 saw momentous victories for the establishment of civil rights by law, yet they were years of crisis for the movement itself and for Martin Luther King's basic strategy in the South. On the national scene, President Johnson signed into law the Voting Rights Act of 1965. Five days later, racial tensions exploded between the police and black residents in the Watts section of Los Angeles. Watts was the beginning of a series of riots in inner cities in 1965–68. This racial unrest coupled with nationwide unemployment among blacks was testimony that the destruction of *de jure* segregation had not alleviated all the chronic ills of African Americans, inside or outside the South. Meanwhile, the advent of a more radical black power movement challenged the nonviolent biracial approach advocated by King and his followers for achieving racial justice. Essential to the black power philosophy was the belief that African Americans had to develop their own strategies to improve their own social and economic status. Their progress could no longer depend upon cooperation with whites and white political leaders.

The civil rights movement was expanding beyond the Southern context of Jim Crow segregation to encompass such issues as unemployment, substandard housing, and institutional racism and discrimination. For the United Methodist Church, the shift presented a considerable challenge that likewise was not restricted to the South. The migration of African Americans from rural to urban areas in the middle decades of the 1900s had altered the residential patterns of many cities. Neighborhoods around many centrally located Methodist churches began to change from all-white to heavily integrated to all-black. Inner-city white churches now had to draw members from a greater distance or follow their members to the suburbs. Most such white churches that chose not to relocate experienced a sharp decline in membership.

In Birmingham, for example, First, Woodlawn, McCoy, South Highlands, and Eastlake Methodist churches—all within older residential areas—began to lose their membership to churches in the newer suburbs of Vestavia, Homewood, and Mountain Brook. Although the Methodist Church was no more responsible than were other denominations for demographic changes, inner-city Methodist congregations began to see that their projects and programs could no longer be devoted to mainly white middle-class members. To survive in their present locations, they would have to concentrate their resources on an urban ministry.[1] Moreover, such a ministry would depend on the total dismantling of institutional barriers within the church.

For Bishop Goodson, the challenge was to accomplish complete merger as quickly as possible. He fully realized that the difficult battle would test his leadership. He wrote in his "Bishop's Corner" column in 1966 that "the only real question" was whether the Central Jurisdiction would be abolished by voluntary action among the annual conferences or by an act mandated from the General Conference."[2] Early in 1967 he called the cabinets of his two white conferences, North Alabama and Alabama-West Florida, to meet in Birmingham with the cabinet of the black Central Alabama Conference. During a two-day session in April, the bishop put in place the structural underpinning for a successful merger vote by establishing representative advisory committees. To coordinate a merger plan, Goodson appointed a Joint Committee on Inter-Conference Relations whose members were ministers from the three Alabama conferences—the highly respected Paul Duffey (chair) from A-WFC, Joseph Lowery from CAC, and Calvin Pinkard from NAC. The difficulty of their task became evident the following June when a resolution to eliminate the denomination's racial structure was defeated 339–312 by NAC and 267–207 by A-WFC.[3] Goodson could no longer harbor expectations that merger could occur without an energetic and carefully planned campaign on the part of his office.

As scheduled, in 1968 Goodson added the Central Alabama Conference to his existing bishoprics of the North Alabama and the Alabama-West

Florida conferences.[4] One of his first actions as the CAC's new bishop was to invite the four black district superintendents and their wives to a meeting at his Vestavia home to meet with the white district superintendents and their spouses. Martha Goodson served the assembled Methodist couples a Southern-style buffet meal as part of the meeting. When one of the black superintendents filled his plate and started toward the back porch to eat, the bishop not only stopped him but escorted him to the main dining room then asked him to offer the blessing. The superintendent was so moved that he could not speak; someone else had to pray over the food.[5]

It was unthinkable that any of his predecessors as bishop might have made such a clear statement of racial openness, but Goodson was willing to challenge Southern social tradition even as he realized how the break would be regarded by the segregationists in his church. Indeed, Goodson was not about to let racial conservatives block his determination to unite the Methodist Church in Alabama. During the next few months, he refined his plans. He began by turning Paul Duffey's Joint Committee on Inter-Conference Relations into the Tri-Conference Advisory Committee on Merger. The new committee's membership contained many individuals, from both the laity and clergy, whom Goodson knew to be sympathetic to merger. The lay members from north Alabama included Harry Denman; prominent Birmingham lawyer Frank Dominick; and Maud Capps, a Gadsden leader in the Women's Society of Christian Service. The ministers from NAC included Denson Franklin, Bert Goodwin, Duncan Hunter, and others who had supported the bishop's efforts; the CAC representatives included Joseph Lowery and Charles Hutchinson. Leo Brannon, a Mobile minister who had become one of Goodson's most important lieutenants, played a key role in the deliberations by transcribing the various discussions and suggestions of committee members. Brannon recalled that in the early sessions it was difficult for the group to focus on a specific strategy.[6]

On the national political scene, 1968 was replete with a succession of unexpected crises. The year began with the apparent failure of the U.S. military effort in Vietnam and the subsequent decision by President Lyndon B. Johnson not to seek reelection. The ensuing debate over the war and a power struggle within the Democratic Party were overshadowed by the assassinations of Martin Luther King Jr. in April and Robert Kennedy in June. Political backlash against the Johnson administration's foreign and domestic programs was heightened by the conservative candidacies of Richard Nixon as Republican Party nominee and Alabama George Wallace at the head of a third-party ticket advocating "law and order."

These events were a backdrop for Goodson's decision to push energetically to end racial separation within his three Alabama conferences. The bishop had hoped that merger might be accomplished by the time he began presiding over the Central Alabama Conference. When this did not occur, he redoubled his efforts to increase personal contact between whites and blacks. He began with what he called the Bishop's Convocation on the Mission of the Church, which brought five hundred Methodists from all corners of the state for a two-day gathering at the Thomas Jefferson Hotel in Birmingham. This was an integrated meeting with CAC clergy and laity representatives sitting alongside their white counterparts. The *Advocate* reported that the attendees would take a "new look" at what it meant to be a Methodist.[7] The bishop was determined to remove the question of race relations from the political context of Alabama's volatile racial history and to place it squarely in the spiritual framework of Christian theology. The design of the meetings included "dialogue groups" in which the attendees could discuss issues involving race relations in Alabama Methodism. Prominent Methodist lay women, including Women's Society of Christian Service leaders Louise Branscomb and Ruby King, were a significant presence in the Jefferson ballroom. The next year, 1969, the convocation featured as a keynote speaker Bishop Richard C. Raines of the Florida Conference, who told the assembly that Methodists in the South had "acquiesced in social attitudes and traditions which had put an artificial burden on every Negro and on many poor whites."[8] The Reverend Bill Davis, then at Guntersville, thought that these convocations mobilized Methodists "to be in sympathy with and support efforts to merge."[9]

ONE AREA OF HIS episcopacy that Goodson especially enjoyed was Camp Sumatanga. Under the direction of the dynamic Nina Reeves, the camp was a summer focal point for youth programs. Conference leaders often utilized

*Nina Reeves at Camp Sumatanga, probably in the 1960s.*

its facilities in sponsoring training sessions. Throughout Camp Sumatanga history, its trustees had carefully guarded the premises as a white enclave in which the only blacks allowed were cooks and maintenance staff. According to Reeves, she had held a few integrated meetings of Methodist young people, but they had to be "underground" in Huntsville and Birmingham rather than at Sumatanga.[10] Although some integrated church groups had asked camp superintendent David Hutto in the past for permission to use the facilities, he always turned them down in accord with the segregationist policies of his supervisory board.[11] In the summer of 1968 Goodson preempted the color line by arranging for the annual School of Christian Mission at Sumatanga to include church education workers from the North Alabama Conference and the Central Alabama Conference. Sunday school teachers of both races spent a week of "fellowship and learning."[12] Later that summer the bishop scheduled a ministerial convocation at Sumatanga attended by approximately three hundred ministers; the keynote speaker was Prince Taylor, the first black bishop of the United Methodist Church (UMC), which had only just been created from the merger of the Methodist Church and the Evangelical United Brethren. The evening after Taylor's appearance, David Hutto's home burned to the ground, and there were rumors throughout the conference that a local KKK chapter had been responsible. But camp director Bert Goodwin blamed a faulty water heater.[13]

Camp Sumatanga was also the site of some integrated Methodist women meetings in 1968. The Women's Society of Christian Service, the primary focus of women's involvement and leadership, held a meeting of church missions at the camp; Myrtle Gordon, president of the NAC branch, recalled her careful planning of the meeting with her counterpart in the Central Alabama Conference, Ruby Walker. A chief issue, according to Gordon, was how the women would be housed. They decided on "a separate wing for the blacks."[14] From the perspective of these early gatherings with black women, Gordon recognized that there was little difference in their points of view, for "we had the same hopes and dreams for the church." The major accomplishment of the meeting was to adopt a "ministry of reconciliation" in the coming year that would "develop pilot projects of dialogue across the barriers that divide communities." The point was to bring together women of "different backgrounds so that attitudes might be changed and understanding increased."[15] Unfortunately, even with Kenneth Goodson as bishop, there were not yet any Alabama women clergy, and although women were allowed to play a role in ceremonial occasions, they were underrepresented on conference committees. Probably the most prominent woman in the conference was Dr. Branscomb, who spoke out consistently in support of merger. The larger community, however, regarded her as a firebrand radical who even advocated the diplomatic recognition of "Red" China.

IN 1969, KENNETH GOODSON received recognition of his leadership on racial relations from the national church. The United Methodist Church established a new Commission on Religion and Race and named Goodson as one of two bishops invited to attend the group's first meeting in Chicago;

the other was Charles F. Golden from the Central Jurisdiction, who as early as 1952 had written the first resolution to the General Conference advocating a racially inclusive church structure.[16] The 1968 General Conference meeting in Dallas had charged the commission with giving "leadership, counsel, and guidance in the whole field of race relations."[17] Behind the scenes, Goodson realized that his appointment to this national body might even make merger in his own conferences more difficult, and he made his acceptance of the post conditional on the simultaneous selection of Duncan Hunter as an at-large member. The Reverend Hunter, whose knowledge of the forces at work both for and against merger in Alabama was authoritative, would be invaluable to Goodson in navigating the difficult months ahead. The segregationist forces within the two white Alabama conferences resented as an unmerited interference in local governance the General Conference's increasing pressure on the Southeastern Jurisdiction to integrate. They would not welcome their own bishop taking a leading role in this process.

For Goodson's part, personal ambition outweighed his fears over any local reaction. This was a difficult and emotional moment for the bishop: he was by now fully aware that segments of his laity would rather leave the church than integrate. As one lay leader told St. Paul's Joseph Lowery, the North Alabama Conference would "sooner merge with Outer Mongolia" than with the Central Alabama Conference.[18]

A measure of Goodson's national stature was his election as president of the new commission, and he told the *Advocate* that he had agreed to a "fearsome responsibility."[19] After his return from Chicago, Goodson charged his clergy and laity to respond to recent social initiatives issued by the April 1968 General Conference meeting in Dallas. There the delegates had sought to recognize the church's responsibility to the inner city and the crisis of the preceding "long hot summer" of racial conflicts and riots in major American urban areas outside the South. The General Conference began a program of "reconciliation" between the United Methodist Church and the inner city. As Goodson explained in one of his "Bishop's Corner" columns, the church wanted to devote a portion of its resources to "constructive social change" and to "assist poor and minority peoples toward . . . genuine self-determination."[20] The approach to racial integration was stressed as the essential social mission of Christianity to the underclass of America. This tactic served as a political weapon intended to disarm the segregationist ranks within Methodism.

In response, some thousand Methodists from all three Alabama conferences attended a Conference on Reconciliation in January 1969 at Birmingham's First United Methodist Church. To launch the initiative, Goodson invited Roy Nichols, a black bishop from Pittsburgh and a member of the Commission on Religion and Race, to preach to the assembled Alabamians. At the end of the session, Goodson called for the three conferences to appoint task forces to study the need for conciliation in the world and the "brokenness of society" in their respective districts and to prepare a plan of action by July 15.[21] A few months later Goodson promised that he would dedicate a portion of the NAC's resources to constructive social change, which included funds for churches in low-income neighborhoods.[22]

THE RECONCILIATION EFFORT IN north Alabama resulted in white and black Methodists working together to create community action programs in the inner city and declining neighborhoods of Birmingham. Undertaken in conjunction with other denominations and existing community public agencies, by the summer of 1969 the effort had styled itself the Greater Birmingham Ministries (GBM). Bill Miles, a young clergyman concerned about local urban poverty, assumed leadership within the North Alabama Conference and centered the GBM's initial outreach programs in the old declining neighborhoods north of downtown. The *Advocate* described the Norwood community ministry as an "agency of *reconciliation*" in an area "broken by contrasting cultures and racial tension."[23] Other new Methodist initiatives in the central city included an evening ministry and children's ministry by Birmingham First church and funding for a chaplain at the University of Alabama Medical Center. Goodson hoped the NAC would give half a million dollars over four years to support the Fund for Reconciliation programs. An editorial in the *Birmingham News* pointed out that the bishop's appeal for this level of funding was not popular in many churches. In fact, the *News* asserted, Goodson had received "letters, phone calls, and threats to withdraw from the church" in response to his new urban agenda.[24] Betty

Copeland, an early GBM volunteer, recalled that when she and Bill Miles went to several suburban churches to publicize their Norwood program, they were met with lukewarm receptions.[25]

As Greater Birmingham Ministries organized, the Tri-Conference Advisory Committee on Merger was entering a crucial phase. The committee had met numerous times over the past year to develop a plan that would result in the approval of merger by all three conferences. This plan was to be presented at the annual conference meetings in the early summer of 1969 and was to prepare the way for a final merger vote in 1970. Goodson depended on Leo Brannon to coordinate the work of the committee and provide staff support for its deliberations. After the sixth meeting of the committee in January 1969, Brannon prepared a position paper for the group. He admitted in the document that the work had been "slow and erratic," but he thought the time had come to concentrate action and arrive at a specific strategy.[26]

Brannon hoped the paper would remain confidential during the discussions and be a talking piece for the committee. During March and April the committee would study his summary of suggestions and come together to prepare a comprehensive strategy. He recognized the group's uphill task and wrote that "vast numbers of laymen and ministers" still did not understand or did not accept the merger effort. Brannon proposed that "small dialogue groups" travel throughout the conferences to acquaint local churches with the plan. The total Tri-Conference Advisory Committee would be present at all three annual conferences in 1969 to answer questions about the merger process.

The task before the merger committee was thus complex and fraught with difficult questions, many of them financial: How could black Methodist ministers be brought into the white conferences on anything approaching equality when the black ministers had no district parsonages and earned a salary that was about a third of their white counterparts?[27] Would the white conferences be expected to correct these inequities from their own pockets? The most heated debates within the white conferences during the following months thus revolved around the issue of pension parity. One letter from a retired Gadsden minister asserted that Central Alabama Conference ministers had no right to expect an annuity rate upon their retirement that would be more than they "have earned in their own conference."[28] An equal pension claim for past years of services by black ministers would mean, according to the writer, that annuity claims of all ministers of the North Alabama Conference would be penalized for the benefit of merger. The disgruntled clergyman concluded by asserting that at least half of the white ministers could not afford to have their pension claims reduced.

Duffey was unsympathetic. Too much was at stake for Methodists to allow mere financial considerations to defeat the idea of merger.[29] In fact, the NAC's Board of Pensions had informed Duffey that the net cost to the conference annuity system for absorbing the relatively small number of black ministers (ninety-two) was only around $20,000. Duffey believed that this was not a prohibitive sum and posed no threat to the security of retired ministers.

Central Alabama Conference clergy, on the other hand, told Duffey that they were fearful that they would just be absorbed into the old white conferences. Joseph Lowery, described by Duncan Hunter as "hard-driving," had sincere reservations about the organizational plans.[30] Lowery wanted a completely new structure for Alabama Methodism: a single conference. The most vocal opposition to this suggestion came from the white Alabama-West Florida delegates who believed that their conference had always been a "step-child" to the North Alabama Conference and wanted to maintain their sovereignty. To Lowery's disappointment, the south Alabama members would not even consider surrendering their autonomy.

IN THE MIDST OF these deliberations, Goodson faced challenges over his role in leading the Commission on Religion and Race. The bishop had agreed in 1969 to arrange for and serve as presiding bishop at the next national meeting of the commission, this time in Birmingham. When this invitation became public, Goodson began to encounter strong opposition to the venue, particularly from such conservatives as Bill Brannon, an insurance executive from Central Park United Methodist, and Harold Martin, executive director of the superannuate homes maintained for retired ministers. Martin was a particularly powerful voice, for he served both as a minister and as a state official on the Alabama Board of Education, a post he had received possibly because of his friendship with Governor George Wallace.[31] Many in the opposition did not want the commission meeting to take place locally, purportedly because they feared that racist groups would provoke violence and disrupt the meeting. Goodson himself wavered, and there was talk that he would withdraw the invitation. To his supporters who favored going ahead, Goodson was merely exhibiting a tendency he had displayed in the past: walking a fine line by upholding national social policies while placating the staunch segregationists in his clergy and laity. This time the advocates of racial justice were anxious to move forward and were quite willing to push the bishop forcefully in that direction.

In the fall of 1969, this group decided to head off any inclination that Goodson might have to cancel the commission meeting scheduled for January 1970. John Rutland, who was by this time pastor at Huntsville's Trinity church, called a number of the most progressive clergy, many of whom were now part of Goodson's cabinet, and urged them to join him in interceding with the bishop. Among those was Claude Whitehead, superintendent of the Florence District, who offered to arrange a meeting with Goodson during an Athens College fundraising trip the bishop would be making to north Alabama. As a guest of the Whiteheads in Florence, Goodson would be conveniently removed from his Birmingham office, and the issue could thus be discussed fully. Rutland's gathering was impressive: four district superintendents (Whitehead, Tom Stevenson, Barry Anderson, and Bob Morgan) and three prominent ministers (Rutland, Paul Clem, and Duncan Hunter). These seven comprised what Whitehead later would describe as the younger establishment of the conference who were "of one mind" as to where the Alabama church ought to go on race relations.[32]

According to Whitehead, their strategy was to avoid confrontation, for Goodson was always sensitive about criticism from his ministers. But with John Rutland leading the conversation, the ministers and laity told the bishop that he could not call off the commission meeting in Birmingham. Goodson seemed surprised by the firmness of their collective advice and, after returning to Birmingham, announced that the meeting would stay in place for early the following year. This was a clear indication that Goodson had decided to stay the course and represented a turning point in his conversations with conservatives. In essence Goodson was announcing that his racial agenda would be the same as that of the national church. From that time on, according to Whitehead, the lay conservatives excluded the bishop from their social invitations, having decided that he was clearly not willing to compromise or slow the process of merger. The participants in the Florence meeting with Goodson became known throughout conservative Methodist circles as the "Dirty Seven."[33]

ON FEBRUARY 9, 1970, thirty-four members of the Commission on Religion and Race were welcomed to Birmingham-Southern College for their national meeting. This gathering came soon after federal court rulings had called for the more forceful desegregation of public schools in the South. Some churches in Alabama had offered their facilities to establish segregated private academies, and the commission members responded by going on record against using church property for "private schools or other activities whose purpose [was] to circumvent the integration of the public schools." Dr. John U. Munro, dean of freshman studies at Birmingham's Miles College (an all-black CME school), spoke to the group at dinner of the need for Methodists to move ahead forcefully on racial issues. The churchmen, he said, would be "remiss not to know the degree to which moderate blacks are fed up" and that the "capital of goodwill between the races" was "slipping away." He urged the church to send more white students to black colleges and to "make friends across racial lines."[34] Made up equally of blacks and whites, the commission also heard a statement of dissent from two members of a new group calling itself the Concerned Methodist Laymen United (CMLU). Based in Ensley, this new organization expressed its opposition to an "interracial conference merger" and deplored the denomination's "liberal trends in literature, social reform and politics." By and large, however, the meeting went well, and Goodson's personal charm and hospitality overcame the commission's initial trepidation about meeting in Birmingham. As one black minister from Beaumont, Texas, remarked, Goodson's welcome at the opening banquet had made him feel differently about Birmingham.[35]

Meanwhile, the tri-conference committee completed its merger plan and sent it to congregations in all three conferences for study. The proposal

brought within the existing boundaries of the two Alabama white conferences all the administrative boards and agencies of the Central Alabama
Conference. The plan recommended that at least one CAC minister be given
a district superintendent post and that other conference staff positions be
integrated. Minimum salaries and pension plans were to be the same for all
conferences, which meant that most black ministers would become full-time
employees of the conferences. The chair of the merger committee, Paul Duffey, assured *Advocate* readers that the new black membership would "bring
assets in persons, property, and dedication." The committee leaders were
careful to point out that the new organizational structure would not affect
the appointment of pastors and that the racial merger of local churches was
a "matter for action on the part of the congregations involved."[36]

Before presentation of the merger proposal to the three conferences for
approval at their annual meetings in October, Goodson mounted an all-
out public relations campaign. Duncan Hunter, a member of the merger
committee, recalled that Goodson directed his district superintendents to
appoint task groups to discuss the tri-conference plan and to consider the
importance of removing racial separation for both theological and practical
considerations.[37]

A report by Claude Whitehead in the spring of 1970 is representative
of the effort in most districts. From Florence, where he was now a district
superintendent, Whitehead sent detailed reports to the bishop outlining the
training of twenty laity and ten clergy to present and advocate the merger
plan in that area. He had also organized a series of monthly meetings in
different churches and had invited Goodson to engage in a two-hour session with those members of Florence First church who were opposed to
merger.[38] Whitehead admitted that he was worried that the newly formed
Concerned Methodist Laymen United would undermine the merger plan.
"I have stated unequivocally my conviction," he wrote Goodson, "that this
is a movement to subvert the church and not a legitimate protest of *good
laymen*." Whitehead's efforts were paralleled in other districts. Bob Morgan,
district superintendent in Tuscaloosa, wrote Goodson in March that he had
met with all the preachers in his district about the plans of the CMLU.[39]
Morgan hoped the conservative lay group would not come to his district

to solicit support, but he was prepared to confront them if they appeared.

Whitehead, Morgan, and other pro-merger ministers hoped that lay leaders would become the most effective defenders of the plan. As Thomas Cunningham, a layman in the Anniston District, wrote other lay leaders in March 1970, they had probably seen mass mailings from the Ensley-based group that attacked merger. Cunningham did not dispute the Concerned Methodist Laymen United's right to speak out, but he believed their intent was to "split asunder the churches of our North Alabama Conference." To this end, Cunningham responded to several points being raised by the plan's critics. On the issue of the expense of bringing the black conference within the white Alabama conferences on an equal economic basis, Cunningham argued that the number of Central Alabama Conference churches amounted to only 92, while the white churches in Alabama numbered 862; further, the national church had promised to help defray the cost of structural integration. More importantly, merger would make possible more "effective ministry" in CAC churches by providing their ministers with adequate salaries and pension plans. The other issue that Cunningham addressed was related directly to the bishop's power to transfer ministers from one church to another within the new combined conferences. Here the implication of the CMLU's propaganda was that Goodson would place black ministers in white churches. The pro-merger lay leaders conceded that he would have every right to do so, but that his doing so was highly unlikely given racial attitudes in most churches. "The bishop has enough headaches without adding this one," Cunningham concluded.[40]

DURING THE FIRST SIX months of 1970, other lay leaders and ministers published letters in the *Advocate* supporting the merger agenda. Most of these testimonies reminded Alabama Methodists that the church's integration was long overdue. The letters also demonstrated that a new generation of Methodists had assumed positions in the most important churches in the conference and were willing to go on record on the issue. Allan D. Montgomery, pastor of Mountain Brook's Canterbury Methodist, wrote that the United Methodist Church had "delayed this step as long as it can. . . . The time for decision has come."[41] A retired member of the North

Alabama Conference, P. D. Wilson, testified to his own personal journey toward racial conciliation: every time "I pray 'Our father' or 'give us this day our daily bread,' I must be acknowledging that the black Christian is my brother."[42] Manley Yielding, a young lawyer who had served on the Greater Birmingham Ministries board, wrote that his experience of working with members from the Central Alabama Conference had convinced him that "merger is not only right, it will work. The hour is already too late and I hope that we will delay no longer."[43]

The *Advocate* was willing to publish letters from anti-merger proponents but informed its readers that the newspaper's position was clearly on the side of the official position of the United Methodist Church on merger. The published letters against racial conciliation from lay Methodists were numerous and decidedly explicit. Henry W. Sweet of Bessemer wrote that "nowhere in the Bible does God advocate forced mixing of the races. . . . He respected local customs and nowhere encouraged intermarriage of races or tribes."[44] Wilbur W. Schou of Wylam warned that the absorption of the black conference would result in the loss of many white members who resented the church's leadership forcing its "extreme liberal trends." Thomas R. Duffey of Birmingham asked, if there were not to be any changes in the conference program or the appointment of "colored" ministers to white churches, then "why merge"? Looking back thirty years later, Duncan Hunter recalled that there were "unbelievable predictions" about what might happen if merger occurred, and he recognized that the real opponents were the "wool hat" crowd: country people, not seminary graduates.[45]

THE MOST IMPORTANT PIECE to appear in the *Advocate* relating to the merger process of the preceding two years was the transcript of an interview by Leo Brannon with Charles L. Hutchinson, pastor of St. Paul United Methodist Church in downtown Birmingham. Within the tri-conference committee, Joseph Lowery had been the most prominent voice of the Central Alabama Conference; now his colleague Hutchinson was emerging as an equally effective spokesman for the African American ministers. Hutchinson offered the first black support in print for a plan that had been largely engineered and directed by the white Methodist establishment. Until then, the views of black United Methodists were largely confined in the *Advocate* to formal reports on CAC meetings. In answer to Brannon's carefully crafted questions on the background of merger, Hutchinson reminded readers that black United Methodists had never wanted the Central Jurisdiction in the first place. Here Hutchinson was responding to one of the CMLU's main attacks on the plan: their allegation that white leadership of the national church was forcing the integration of the conferences against the will of African American Methodists, that the General Conference was "cramming it down their throats." Hutchinson believed this rumor indicated that whites just did not want to be reconciled to an organization plan with blacks included. "We have always wanted inclusiveness," Hutchinson maintained, "and this separateness is not in keeping with the Gospel of our Lord."

While the black Birmingham minister admitted that the CAC official hierarchy would probably "lose some positions of power and influence" as a result of merger, this was a price that they would pay "for the sake of inclusiveness." He remembered that his original fears that the tri-conference committee process would be dominated by whites had proved groundless and that true dialogue had taken place between whites and blacks in numerous meetings. Hutchinson had been happily surprised when representatives of both races sat down and worked together. The result was that "many things happen when you begin to know people for what they are." What if the white conferences defeated merger? He thought that the result would be a feeling of "alienation" in the black community that would permanently impair racial relations within the denomination. Hutchinson concluded by saying that his hope and dream was that blacks and whites would worship and work together and that there would be no exclusion by race in any church.[46]

The Central Alabama Conference had been moving toward approval of the merger plan when conference leaders unanimously endorsed the plan in a meeting at St. Paul UMC in late March of 1970. At the annual meeting, held June 17 in Mobile, Bishop Goodson again presided, and Paul Duffey answered questions from the assembled delegates. District Superintendent Charles Hutchinson spoke eloquently for the plan. Part of his speech was a strong statement of how he believed the civil rights struggle applied to the church. His support of merger was "not to be with the white man or sit beside him in his church, but to be aware that the pressure of God and this hour is upon us. God has called us in this hour to be brothers. . . . Our white brother has coined a definition of what it means to be human and has left the black man out of his definition. We are human like they are. They have us on their hands in a sense, and by our stand and vote today, we don't intend to let the white man get off the hook that easy."[47]

Most but not all of the delegates used the occasion to voice their support for the merger plan. One delegate questioned whether merger would have a desirable effect if it succeeded in driving out 200,000 whites. Others were concerned that once their conference approved merger, the details of the plan might then be altered by the two white conferences in their sessions. Duffey was quick to say that any changes would have to be presented to all three conferences. In the end, the CAC decided to forego a secret ballot, and a standing vote resulted in 149 delegates on their feet for the merger with no votes cast against merger. Goodson, always an emotional person at these events, was overwhelmed and told the conference that he could "see the Holy City." A fitting end to the occasion was a rousing singing by all assembled of "We Shall Overcome."[48]

However, merger faced tough opposition in the two white conferences. When the North Alabama Conference held its 1970 annual meeting at Birmingham-Southern College on June 7, Bishop Goodson presented tri-conference co-chair Paul Duffey, who read the report, and the Reverend R. Laurence Dill Jr., who moved its acceptance. A vigorous debate then developed on the floor of the conference between proponents and opponents of the plan. After a secret ballot of the delegates was taken, the ballots were counted the next day. The merger plan had lost by 28 votes—431 votes in favor and 459 against. In the Alabama-West Florida Conference, the plan failed by an even wider margin of 72 votes on June 4.[49]

As Goodson reported in his column in July, the Central Alabama Conference experience had been "almost too much a good thing for many of us who were present." Despite the setback in the two white conferences, he promised to continue his plan to "implement the policy and stated program of the United Methodist Church" by ending all "structures based upon race."

The bishop spent the rest of 1970 steadily working to change the minds of those who had voted against merger. He repeatedly reminded his constituency of the importance of complying with the goals of the national church. "I've got enough sense to know that race is the crucial issue of our time," he told his *Advocate* readers. "If the church can't discuss race, and if it can't be resolved in the community of the faithful, then where on earth can we turn in this world?"[50] During the months that remained until the next year's annual conferences, Goodson made the merger proposal the subject of various appearances and Sunday sermons throughout the state. His determination to settle the issue may be seen in his letter to a minister who had appeared at the CAC session in Mobile. "If we don't land this time," he wrote in reference to the passage of merger, "we'll keep circling that field until every enemy plane has taken off and we can land in peace."[51] The bishop continued to believe that he could persuade a few segregationists in his two white conferences to swing to the other side, and it was said that behind the scenes he was even trying to persuade G. Stanley Frazer to support merger.[52]

The Tri-Conference Advisory Committee reconvened in mid-January 1971 to consider "Where do we go from here?" Their discussions centered on such alternatives as modifying the plan and postponing the proposal for another year. In the end, with a strong push from Duffey and Goodson, the committee decided to resubmit the plan without alterations at the next annual conference sessions. Again the group saturated the two white conferences with a pro-merger campaign that included appearances by committee members in their own districts' pulpits in February and March to discuss the plan and answer questions. Utilizing the latest technology, the committee provided tape cassettes of questions and answers pertaining to merger for use in local churches. Small groups of blacks and whites were organized to meet in sessions to discover "what feelings exist between the two over the question of merger."[53] To provide the maximum time for favorable lobbying at the annual conferences, the plan of merger was to be presented late in the sessions, perhaps on the next to the last day.

The June 1971 meeting of the North Alabama Conference took place in a packed Munger Hall on the Birmingham-Southern campus. Nina Reeves recalled that the mood in the hall was "very tense, especially in an auditorium with inadequate air conditioning."[54] Ed Montgomery, lay delegate from Tuscaloosa, noted that the well-represented Concerned Methodist Laymen United had "stirred up a lot of resistance, even on the final day of the vote."[55] The CMLU had been particularly efficient in mobilizing opposition to the plan from the small, mainly blue-collar churches to the west of downtown Birmingham. South Highlands United Methodist in the city was still a forceful advocate of a segregated church and several senior members of that congregation spoke against merger. On the other hand, those ministers and lay leaders who favored the plan were vocal as well. Odie Gregg, a lay delegate, spoke for merger, quoting Martin Luther: "Here I stand; I can do no other." Ted Leach, a young minister from Vestavia, recalled that when one of the older ministers asked, "How many of you would be willing to serve a black church," he "proudly" stood up in the crowded balcony to show his response.[56] Bert Goodwin, the new director of Camp Sumatanga, recalled being told that a building at the camp was on fire, but he didn't leave to see about it because he wanted to vote for merger.[57] Methodist young people were also at the conference and supported merger. The president of the conference's Methodist Youth Fellowship, June Morgan, would not leave until the vote was taken.[58]

When the votes were tallied, the delegates had approved the merger by a single vote, 429 to 428. The Reverend Bob Morgan recalled that Goodson ordered him to recount the votes because the razor-thin outcome "scared him to death."[59] "Have them go count it again," the bishop told him, "because I'm afraid to announce this." The recount resulted in the same difference of one vote. Morgan also remembered that while Goodson was "terribly disappointed" at the closeness of the numbers, he went on to address the conference very directly, telling them: "It's passed and it doesn't make any difference if it was one vote or a thousand." Those who had voted against the proposal were so disappointed that they subsequently started rumors that their bishop had rigged the vote. Conversely, many in attendance later claimed that their one vote had made the difference.[60]

GOODSON WAS CLEARLY PLEASED that the northern half of Alabama Methodism was now in compliance with the national church's mandate. He admitted the battle had not been easy. Before his arrival in Alabama, some courageous younger clergy had supported removal of racial barriers within the church and the destruction of the state's segregation system. But they had almost no chance of success until the Methodist hierarchy above them shifted. Thus the assignment of Goodson to the North Alabama episcopacy was a turning point for Methodism in the state. Goodson, though not a doctrinaire advocate of racial equality, was a leader who moved toward the support of civil rights, just as other white Southerners of his generation were doing. Goodson recognized that the continuation of segregation within the church was a fundamental moral wrong. He always believed that a polite and non-confrontational approach to the segregationists would persuade them of the rightness of integration.

Outright confrontation with the segregationist forces eventually did emerge in Goodson's strategy, but not before he had tried other avenues of consultation and communication with the other side. One part of Goodson's strategy was to engineer the merger plan without much direct involvement by black ministers from the Central Conference in Alabama. Nor did Goodson ever go beyond his advocacy of integration of the conferences to a much more explosive issue—the possibility that individual church congregations could now be integrated. His approach was that of a moderate, and he believed that this was the only avenue that would work effectively in Alabama. Goodson viewed his term on the Commission on Religion and Race as a time in which he came to a fundamental understanding of the price the church was paying for an organizational structure based on racial separation. "I did not realize the extent to which it would allow me to sense the real feelings and hear the real cries and pleas of the minority groups who are within United Methodism," he wrote in the *Advocate*. The most important outcome to Goodson was that African Americans could now "hear our preachments on brotherhood and human dignity" and believe them.[61]

Goodson had to wait another year for a favorable vote in the Alabama-West Florida Conference. It came on May 30, 1972, with a vote of 363 for merger and 182 against. By that time, his days in Alabama were numbered. He had served nearly eight years in the state and he would soon be the senior bishop in the Southeastern Jurisdiction. Although the two conferences

*Bishops Kenneth Goodson and Carl J. Sanders, 1960s.*

requested that he be reassigned to Alabama, the General Conference assigned him to the episcopacy in Richmond, Virginia, nearer to his North Carolina roots. The new Alabama bishop, Carl J. Sanders, arrived that summer, and he presided over the formal ceremony on October 24, 1972, that brought the three conferences together. At the specially called session in Birmingham's new civic auditorium, Sanders read to the assembly a telegram from Kenneth Goodson of good wishes and greetings which closed with the words of one of his favorite hymns, "In Christ, there is no East or West."[62]

## NOTES

1. It would not be easy to attract African Americans to join a formerly all-white congregation, and even more difficult to persuade white membership to embrace the concept of a biracial church community.

2. *Alabama Christian Advocate*, November 1, 1966. The bishop's cabinet within a conference referred to all of the district superintendents and the head of the Council on Ministries. This comprised a body that met in regular and special sessions to advise the bishop on conference matters.

3. Ibid., June 13, 1967.

4. That same year, 1968, the official name of the Methodist denomination became the United Methodist Church (UMC); this change represented the joining of a much smaller Methodist group, the Evangelical United Brethren, with the much larger main body of the church. From this point on, "United Methodist Church" became part of the official name of most Methodist congregations (e.g., Bessemer United Methodist Church).

5. Mitchell, *Election*, 35.

6. Leo Brannon, "Study Document for the Tri-Conference Advisory Committee on Merger," March 18, 1969. Typescript in NACA 6.2, Bishops' Papers.

7. *Alabama Christian Advocate*, January 30, 1968.

8. Ibid., July 1, 1969.

9. Davis interview tape, May 9, 2001, Robinson, NACA.

10. Reeves interview tape, May 7, 2001, NACA..

11. Mitchell, "We Are at our Best," 34.

12. *Alabama Christian Advocate*, July 1, 1968.

13. Bert Goodwin interview, Nicholas, May 13, 2002, NACA.

14. Myrtle Gordon interview, Nicholas, March 4, 1996, NACA.

15. *Alabama Christian Advocate*, February 25, 1969.

16. Murray, *Methodists*, 62.

17. *Alabama Christian Advocate*, September 3, 1968.

18. Quoted in interview with Elmore, Nicholas.

19. *Alabama Christian Advocate*, November 19, 1968.

20. Ibid., March 4, 1969.

21. Ibid., January 14, 1969.

22. Ibid., April 8, 1969.

23. Ibid. Norwood had once been one of the city's most fashionable neighborhoods with many imposing homes, but white flight to the suburbs in the 1940s and 1950s had left it an area of extreme poverty, considerable crime, and urban blight, with many of the homes vacant and deteriorating.

24. *Birmingham News*, June 7, 1969.

25. Betty Copeland interview, Nicholas, February 27, 1996, NACA.

26. Brannon, "Study Document," NACA 6.3, Bishops' Papers.

27. "A Summary of the Relation of the Central Alabama Conference to the Alabama-West

Florida Conference," n.d., NACA 6.2, Bishops' Papers.

28. Thomas A. Edgar to Duffey, November 12, 1969, NACA 6.2, Bishops' Papers.

29. Duffey to Edgar, January 15, 1970, NACA 6.2, Bishops' Papers.

30. Tape of Duncan Hunter interview, April 25, 2001, Robinson, NACA.

31. Don Neal interview, Nicholas, June 15, 2009. Harold Martin in his ministerial capacity was a district superintendent on two occasions and was at this time the executive director of the Conference's 115 superannuate homes for retired Methodist ministers. He oversaw pensions and retirement homes, and was responsible for building a number of new retirement facilities throughout northern Alabama. Martin was completely opposed to the integration of the conferences, and, according to a then-young minister in the NAC, had been a long-time friend and confidant of George Wallace. For a summary of Martin's later years, see "A Lifetime of Giving Continues: Maintaining the Momentum." https://www.uab.edu/give/campaign/winter-2011 (accessed May 28, 2017).

32. Claude Whitehead interview, June 2, 2003, Nicholas NACA.

33. Elmore interview tape, April 6, 2001, Robinson. NACA. "Dirty Seven" probably referred to the fact that these ministers were considered the most radical of the clergy in their push for merger, and seems to question their tactics. The phrase, coined by their detractors, soon became a badge of honor.

34. *Alabama Christian Advocate*, February 24, 1970. John U. Munro had a remarkable career. In 1967, Munro, then dean of Harvard College, astonished his colleagues by resigning and moving to Miles College, a cash-strapped, unaccredited, historically black college on the outskirts of Birmingham. There Munro designed and directed the freshman studies program and taught writing and social science. He brought student volunteers from Harvard in the summer of 1964 to team with Miles students in a grade-school tutoring project. Once he moved to Miles, he continued to recruit graduate students and young teachers to the South, while maintaining that black colleges required black leadership to fulfill their mission. He remained at Miles for ten years and them moved to Tougaloo College, another historically black school in northern Mississippi, where he taught for almost twenty more years. See Toni Lee Camposella, "John Usher Munro, Brief Life of an Uncommon Educator, 1912–2002" *Harvard Magazine*. http://harvardmagazine.com/2013/05/vita-john-usher-Munro. (Accessed May 29, 2017).

35. *Alabama Christian Advocate*, February 17, 24, 1970.

36. Ibid., February 17, January 20, February 3, 1970.

37. Hunter interview tape, April 25, 2001, Robinson, NACA.

38. Memorandum by Claude Whitehead, n.d., NACA 6.2, Bishops' Papers.

39. Morgan to Goodson, March 4, 1970, NACA 6.2, Bishops' Papers.

40. Thomas Cunningham to Anniston lay leaders, March 4, 1970, NACA 6.2, Bishops' Papers.

41. *Alabama Christian Advocate*, March 3, 1970.

42. Ibid., March 10, 1970.

43. Ibid., March 31, 1970.

44. Ibid., April 28, 1970.

45. Hunter interview tape, April 25, 2001, Robinson, NACA.

46. *Alabama Christian Advocate*, April 7, 1970.

47. *Daily Proceedings of the Ninety-fifth Annual Session of the Central Alabama Conference of the United Methodist Church 1970*, NACA.

48. *Alabama Christian Advocate*, July 7, 1970.

49. *Alabama Christian Advocate,* June 9, 1970.

50. Ibid., October 27, 1970.

51. Goodson to Warren M. Jenkins, April 13, 1970, NACA 6.2, Bishops' Papers.

52. Mitchell, "We Are at Our Best," 35.

53. "Minutes of the Meeting of the Tri-Conference Advisory Special Committee, January 26, 1971," NACA.

54. Reeves interview tape, May 7, 2001, Robinson, NACA.

55. Montgomery interview tape, April 11, 2001, NACA.

56. Tape of Ted Leach interview tape, April 25, 2001, NACA.

57. *Birmingham News*, October 14, 1990.

58. Reeves interview tape, May 7, 2001, Robinson, NACA.

59. Morgan interview tape, May 9, 2001, NACA.

60. One often-repeated, but possibly apocryphal, story is that a prominent businessman in the lay delegation, Elton B. Stephens, had left the auditorium to use the restroom when the vote was taken, and he most certainly would have voted against merger, resulting in a tied vote.

61. *Alabama Christian Advocate*, September 28, 1971.

62. It would appear from the lack of any written evidence that Sanders did not invite Goodson to be present at the formal ceremony of merger.

*The first issue of the Alabama Methodists' newspaper after the merger, June 1972.*

# V.

# An Achievement of Sorts, 1972–1990

The transition from Bishop Kenneth Goodson to Bishop Carl Sanders was not only abrupt but a step backwards in leadership on the merger issue. Sanders had a much less open style of leadership and was determined to do things his own way. At the beginning of his episcopacy he decided not to invite Goodson to the October meeting that formalized merger. Goodson's supporters were disappointed that Sanders did not include the former bishop in a program that would have recognized what had been Goodson's greatest accomplishment. More significantly, the new bishop began to exclude Goodson's district superintendents from the decision-making process, particularly in regard to the merger transition. The merger plan had called for at least one African American superintendent, and Bob Morgan recalled that Charles Hutchinson and John Norwood were the most likely candidates.[1] During his first few months in office, Bishop Sanders appointed Hutchinson to the NAC Council on Ministries, but he then waited an entire year to appoint a black district superintendent. When the cabinet met in 1974 to consider ministerial and district appointments, Sanders displayed a considerably different style of administrative approach from the open and receptive personality of Goodson. Bob Morgan, who was serving as secretary to the cabinet, recalled that Sanders just called out the names of his appointments, including Moses C. Barrett as the new superintendent for the Decatur district. This name was unknown to the attendees; later they learned that Barrett had been serving in a small black church in the Alabama-West Florida Conference and lacked only a few years before retirement. Morgan compared the appointment to "taking someone out of an elementary school and putting them with tenured faculty."[2] What seems clear is that Sanders passed over the most dynamic and talented black leadership from the old Central Alabama Conference to name a man who would not "champion the cause of racial relations" within the new integrated conferences.[3] The episode also indicated that Sanders was oblivious to the black ministers' concerns, expressed during the merger talks, that they would be relegated to minor roles of leadership in the newly configured conference structure.

The black ministers and laity who entered the white conferences in 1972 needed a bishop who would support the process of integration as vigorously as Goodson had done. However, other than the organizational shift, a Methodist visitor from outside Alabama would have seen little racial mixing in the North Alabama Conference during the 1970s. Sanders, whatever his personal beliefs, did nothing to encourage the integration of individual congregations, and he certainly never considered assigning a black minister to head a white congregation. Duncan Hunter thought that the momentum of the Goodson years was quickly lost. As district superintendent in Anniston in 1976, he found it difficult to get new black leadership in a church that was now controlled by a white majority.[4] At Camp Sumatanga, the youth program after merger recruited few black children for integrated summer sessions because, according to Nina Reeves, the black churches wanted camps for their own race.[5] Black Methodists also missed the sense of community that they had known in terms of district and conference meetings in the old separate jurisdiction.[6] At the beginning of 1974, Anniston pastor George L. Russell commented in the *Advocate* that although the anticipated wholesale departure of black and white members had not happened, the Central Alabama Conference had been more "absorbed than merged."[7]

The women's organizations proved to be the only area of the conference that achieved interracial union. Women from all three conferences met at Sumatanga in January of 1973. Since they had already been meeting together in various settings, Eva Walker, a prominent member of the Women's Society of Christian Service, recalled no feelings of discomfort among the attendees.[8] At the meeting, women from the Society and the Wesleyan Service Guild joined in a "Service of Celebration." The program included a workshop entitled "Include Me In," and for the first time an integrated slate

*Right: From left, Ernest T. Dixon Jr., resident bishop of the Kansas Area; O. Eugene Slater, president of the Council of Bishops of the United Methodist Church and resident bishop of the San Antonio Area; and Carl J. Sanders, resident bishop of the Birmingham Area, receive the Plan of Merger for the United Methodist Church and the Birmingham Area from the Tri-Conference Advisory Committee of the Alabama-West Florida, Central Alabama, and North Alabama Conferences on October 24, 1972, at the Birmingham-Jefferson Civic Center.*

*Top: Bishop Sanders, at the podium, declares "that the Alabama-West Florida Annual Conference, the Central Alabama Annual Conference, and the North Alabama Annual Conference are now merged into two new Annual Conferences to be known as the Alabama-West Florida Annual Conference and the North Alabama Annual Conference." The Declaration, according to the Plan of Merger adopted by the three conferences in annual sessions, came at 12:03 p.m., October 24, 1972, at the Birmingham-Jefferson Civic Center.*

of officers was elected to represent the two organizations. Many women of both races resented that gender discrimination was such a strong force in the church. It was still the practice that only one woman, usually the head of the Women's Society of Christian Service, was sent as a delegate to General Conference meetings. Betty Copeland, active with Greater Birmingham Ministries at this time, recalled that many found Bishop Sanders hostile and condescending to women.[9] In a sense, women and black ministers of the 1970s had much in common; both groups were petitioning for larger roles in local leadership. During that decade, there was little opportunity for women to enter seminary with hope of a ministry within the United Methodist Church. Even as merger was achieved, Methodist women were looking to the church to offer them the same attention that had been afforded African Americans during their civil rights crusade.

THE STRUGGLE TO END the segregated structure of Alabama Methodism both gratified and disappointed its leaders. The participants typically assessed the merger of the CAC into the two white Alabama conferences in terms of the General Conference's mandates and their own personal expectations. However, a fuller assessment and understanding of the Alabama Methodists' situation emerges when they are compared with other Protestant denominations. From the mid-1950s through the early 1970s, other religious leaders in the state similarly confronted the social and theological issues raised by the civil rights movement. Alabama's Southern Baptists, Presbyterians, and Episcopalians underwent a lengthy period of discussion and even conflict over their segregated structures and the implications of integration.

The majority of Alabama's Christians were Baptists (Methodists were the next most numerous). The Baptist numbers were little short of astonishing. In 1965, during the height of the civil rights movement, Baptists were more than half of Alabama's white Christians and nearly half of its African Americans were Baptists. However, they were rigidly segregated. The majority of white Baptists were affiliated with the Southern Baptist Convention (SBC), while black Baptists belonged to one of three black Baptist groups. The connection between black and white Baptists amounted to little more than contributions by individual white churches of small amounts of money to a variety of black Baptist causes and institutions.[10] The numbers of white Southern Baptists meant they had corresponding influence in the state's power structure, and the annual SBC state convention steadfastly defended segregation throughout the 1960s. Historian Mark Newman observed that during the civil rights era the SBC consistently lagged behind other large Christian denominations in the number and content of its pronouncements on race relations.[11] This was certainly true in Alabama, and historian Wayne Flynt, the foremost chronicler of Alabama Baptist history, has suggested that Southern Baptists were no different from whites in general in suffering from a "structural blindness" to how blacks were treated in the state.[12]

Although Governor George Wallace was a Methodist, some of his most enthusiastic supporters were within the Southern Baptist leadership. Dr. Henry L. Lyon Jr., a pastor of one of Montgomery's largest Baptist churches, was a Wallace friend and gave the invocation at his 1963 inauguration.[13] *Alabama Baptist* editor Leon Macon editorialized strongly in support of Wallace's stands on segregation and wrote to him privately in 1965: "You are continuing to make us an excellent Governor and I hope to speak a good word for you over the state if you run for United States Senator."[14] Given this level of support for Wallace's political stance, it is not surprising that Alabama's Southern Baptists kept silent on the state's racial problems. Not until the 1970s did the denomination begin to discuss openly the spiritual problems of maintaining a segregated system. This is not to say that no Baptists advocated an end to the racial divide in the 1960s, but they were outnumbered and their opinions suppressed if they attempted to voice their views within their churches. In fact, a sharp division within a Baptist congregation over racial policy might lead to a significant number of members withdrawing from a church to establish their own church.[15] The Southern Baptist Convention had no authority to intervene.

In contrast, the context of policy and decision-making in Methodism had certain similarities to two other important Protestant groups in Alabama: the Presbyterian Church in the United States (PCUS) and the Episcopalians. Both of these denominations had hierarchical structures similar to Methodism that did not leave congregational authority under the control of individual churches as the Baptists did.

Among the Methodists, Episcopals, and Presbyterians, PCUS (the Presbyterian equivalent of the Methodist Episcopal Church, South) had the most congregation-centered structure. In theory, power flowed upward within the Calvinist order from the presbytery (individual church) through the synod to the General Assembly. In practice, however, the system tended to work in the reverse, and the Presbyterian's highest court often fulfilled the same function as the national Methodist General Conference in setting the norms for theological interpretation and organizational structure. But the main difference in the two bodies was an important one: the Presbyterian General Assembly's authority on significant policy shifts was subject to the strictly voluntary acquiescence of the presbyteries. Like the Methodists, the Presbyterians had split over the issue of slavery, but while the Methodists reunited in 1939, formal reunification of the Presbyterians would wait until 1983. Meanwhile, the Presbyterians debated the pros and cons of segregation as well as a spectrum of other views from liberal to conservative. Also like the Methodists, the PCUS retained a small group of black Presbyterians who worshipped in segregated churches and were excluded from significant leadership positions.[16] The differences over race within the presbyteries also resembled those in the Methodist Church on a number of issues: the admittance of blacks to white worship services, the integration of meetings at the denomination's conference ground in Montreat, North Carolina, and the question of how the church should view the civil disobedience advocated by Martin Luther King Jr. and the SCLC.

For Presbyterians, the points of crisis in the 1960s centered on the pace of integration within the PCUS and the ties that the denomination had with the National Council of Churches. On the first point, an organized movement within the denomination, comparable to the Methodist Federation for Social Action, advocated full equality for African American Presbyterians. This group, the Fellowship of Concern, consisted of Southern Presbyterian clergy and laity who thought the General Assembly was not acting quickly enough on racial reconciliation. Recalcitrant lay leaders formed a conservative group, the Concerned Presbyterians, which like the Concerned Methodist Laymen United's program, tried to prevent integration of the synods. In 1964, with the strong support of the Fellowship of Concern members and Presbyterians outside the South, the General Assembly requested that black churches be absorbed into the geographic presbyteries in the synods of Alabama, Georgia, and Louisiana. The reaction was mixed; some synods complied and others displayed reluctance bordering on hostility.[17] The situation turned into a power struggle between the General Assembly and the non-compliant presbyteries on the grounds that the national organization had no legal authority to force the synods to integrate.

The involvement of Presbyterian officials in the National Council of Churches was an equally acrimonious issue, for Southern Presbyterian traditionalists believed that the political activism of this national organization was in fact influenced by external communist intentions to create social unrest in the segregated South. As in the Methodist experience, there was a distinct difference between the viewpoint of the clergy and the laity, and only a few Presbyterian clergy chose to counter their congregations' resistance to integration. One notable exception was Edward V. Ramage, minister of Birmingham First Presbyterian Church, who like Denson Franklin at Birmingham First Methodist, was willing to allow African American visitors to attend his services. In a much-publicized episode on Easter Sunday, 1963, Ramage welcomed two black women whose entry into the church had almost halted the service, and he invited them to come again. One irate segregationist member afterwards accused Ramage of being a communist, and the minister subsequently had to endure hate threats and a bitter debate within his congregation over racial issues. The increasing pressure on Ramage and his family led him to leave First Presbyterian voluntarily the following fall because he feared that his open-door policy would result in the permanent division of the congregation.

Ramage, a cosigner of the group of eight white ministers' 1963 letter to Martin Luther King Jr., had hoped to resolve the conflict between segregationists and more moderate laity in his church, but in the end his own inner turmoil destroyed his will to stay at his post.[18] His realization that no compromise was possible between the factions at First Presbyterian was a harbinger of a more permanent division within Presbyterian ranks. In 1973, conservative forces within the congregation gathered at Birmingham's Briarwood Presbyterian Church and formed a new denomination, the Presbyterian Church in America, on the grounds that the PCUS had abandoned the Bible and based its authority on human reason and not divine will.[19] In the end, the conservative forces chose the same path that some of their Southern Baptist counterparts had followed: complete separation as a means of avoiding racial togetherness.

In contrast to the Presbyterian's less-centralized organizational structure, the Episcopalians had a prescribed chain of authority that emulated the Roman Catholic structure, from a presiding bishop down to regional diocesan units (each with a bishop) over the individual parish churches. This centralized authority and the fact that the Protestant Episcopal Church had not split over slavery should have made progress on racial matters simpler for the denomination. But within the Episcopalian political structure, black communicants mostly attended separate churches and remained in a distinctly subordinate position. One reflection of this racial divide was that the Episcopal church steadily lost African American membership in the first half of the twentieth century. Less than 2 percent of urban churches in the United States were affiliated with the denomination; outside the cities this figure was less than 1 percent.[20]

Episcopalian Southern dioceses maintained a *de facto* system of segregated convocations and parishes for their black members, and they generally ignored the post-Civil War admonitions of the national church to engage in missionary work among African Americans in their areas. Following the 1954 *Brown* decision, the ensuing civil rights movement intensified conflicts over racial attitudes and policies within Episcopal ranks nationwide. As in the Methodist experience, national church authorities actively advocated racial justice as part of the fundamental message of Christian theology. In Episcopal seminaries, a younger generation of students and faculty were influenced by the writings of German theologian Dietrich Bonhoeffer on the church's relationship to human suffering in the secular world and the congruence of his theology with the traditional Anglican emphasis on the Incarnation.[21] By 1959 an interracial group had formed the Episcopal Society for Cultural and Racial Unity to promote racial integration as part of the official agenda of the church. Led by Atlanta priest John Morris, the group actively participated in the direct action crusades of the SCLC and other African American groups. Episcopalian priests and laity, mainly from outside the South, joined freedom rides in 1961 to integrate public facilities in Louisiana, Mississippi, and Alabama. The 1965 Selma March in support of voting rights drew more than five hundred Episcopalians, and approximately 10 percent of all Episcopalian clergy in the country.[22]

Charles C. J. Carpenter, Bishop of the Diocese of Alabama, reacted vociferously against this involvement by his denomination in civil rights demonstrations of any kind.[23] Carpenter, a man of many contradictions, believed in racial justice as an ideal of Christian behavior, but at the same time he displayed a strong nostalgia for the South's "Lost Cause" and wanted to maintain segregation for the time being to preserve the prevailing social order. Carpenter's words from the pulpit often conflicted with his public denunciations of the Episcopal priests and seminarians that participated in the freedom rides. His greatest wrath was centered on the priests who joined Martin Luther King Jr. in the march to Montgomery. He called the Selma protest "a foolish business and sad waste of time" and announced that those who were priests had no authority to wear clerical clothing in the marches or to represent the Protestant Episcopal Church in those events.[24]

When Jonathan Daniels, a seminarian in Cambridge, Massachusetts, came to Selma and was subsequently murdered in adjacent Lowndes County, Bishop Carpenter made no public comment, even after the murderer was acquitted by an all-white jury. Carpenter's attempts to police the ranks of his own clergy included the banishment of a young priest, Francis X. Walter, from a parish in Eufaula, Alabama, because of Walter's connections with John Morris and the Society for Cultural and Racial Unity.[25] Carpenter and his bishop coadjutor, George Murray, joined Methodist bishops Nolan Harmon and Paul Hardin and other religious leaders in writing the public letter to King in 1963 asking him to cancel his planned demonstrations in the city. Harmon and Carpenter were angry over King's response to their attempt to prevent what they feared would be social disorder and violence if King's agenda in Birmingham went forward. In the end, Carpenter found himself fighting a holding action against social change and facing criticism of his record on racial justice from both sides. For the most part, Carpenter maintained absolute control over his diocese despite the position of the national church. His long tenure as bishop of Alabama, 1938–1969, meant that the Episcopal Church in the state saw little progress on integration during the period when Kenneth Goodson was beginning to move Alabama Methodism toward racial merger.

All these predominantly white Protestant denominations experienced the same social pressures and conflicts in the Alabama setting as the Methodists did. In general the Southern Baptists, Southern Presbyterians, and Episcopalians reflected within their congregations a strong reluctance to change the racial status quo. Whether this change meant school integration or access to public facilities or a racially mixed population on Sunday morning, the usual reaction among whites was resistance and hostility to any alteration of the social order. All of these denominations had clergy who realized the inconsistency of Christian principles with racial exclusion, but their ability to open the minds of their congregations to racial conciliation was limited by a combination of difficult barriers. Most white Southerners of the 1950s and 1960s had grown up in a world in which legal and social segregation was an intrinsic part of their daily lives. For many, superior racial status defined part of who they were as human beings. To challenge this identity from the pulpit was to damage one's credibility as an ordained minister of the church. As the Reverend Ramage observed after he left First Presbyterian and relocated to Texas, the easiest way to end a ministry was to "get out of line on theological or social issues."[26] It was much simpler to ignore the subject of racial discrimination. This was possible within the Southern Baptist and Southern Presbyterian pulpits because local authorities could successfully thwart any pronouncements or policy statements from the Southern Baptist Convention or the PCUS General Assembly. If change came in these two denominations, their political structure seemed to accommodate separation altogether by non-compliant member churches. In theory, the Protestant Episcopal Church at General Convention could decide to absorb black parishes in Alabama into the white churches. This did not happen, partly because of the long-established authority of Bishop Carpenter, who committed a considerable part of his energies to resisting pressure from his national church. It must also be admitted that Carpenter had the support of many black Episcopalians in the South who wanted to maintain their separate church gatherings and parish identities. This situation sharply contrasted with the black conferences within the Methodist Church, who were enthusiastic about merger and anxious to do away with the 1939 segregated version of the Methodist order.

Bishop Goodson's achievement of merger in both white conferences by 1972 thus stands in sharp contrast to the factionalism and gradualism displayed by Alabama's other major Protestant sects. The General Conference of the Methodist Church had mandated dissolution of the Central conferences in 1964 and then had attempted to outflank recalcitrant Southern churches by moving ahead on complete merger despite the declared opposition of the Southeastern Jurisdiction. But Alabama Methodists under the leadership of the bishops prior to 1964, particularly Hodge and Harmon, had moved so slowly that virtually no change occurred. The key to Methodist merger and a significant change in racial attitudes among their clergy and at least a significant portion of the laity in the post-1964 period was Kenneth Goodson's coming to the state, and his extraordinary ability to lead Alabama's Methodist establishment in a different direction.

From the beginning of his episcopacy, Goodson was a good learner and listener. Perhaps he realized that his background from outside the Deep South made him considerably more open to accepting African Americans as equals. As Mark Newman pointed out in his study of Southern Baptists and desegregation, most racial progressives had spent all or part of their childhoods in areas where few blacks lived and overt racism was less marked.[27] Goodson faced a different racial landscape in Alabama than in the mountains of his boyhood home in western North Carolina. He also displayed a markedly different temperament from the formal and old-fashioned clerical personalities of the more elderly bishops who preceded him in Alabama. Goodson was a person of strong physical constitution who loved people. He relished going out into the north Alabama hinterlands where he could deliver colorful, folksy sermons to unsophisticated congregations. Afterwards the bishop and Mrs. Goodson would be a part of that Methodist tradition of Sunday dinner on the lawn with fried chicken, congealed salads, and those banana cream and chocolate pies that Goodson adored. Yet his immediacy and warm personality, however sincere, did not prevent him from speaking his mind on the issues that faced his conferences on the merger question after his first year in office. Goodson was a bishop who viewed his own authority as subservient to the will of the General Conference. His sense of the social theology of his denomination was also totally consistent with the *Discipline* of the Methodist Church. He was fully aware that racism as practiced in Alabama was incompatible with the direction his church was moving in post-World War II America. He was also aware that his job was to enable his two conferences to achieve merger with the Central Alabama Conference as quickly and as smoothly as possible.

Goodson was no political activist, unlike some of his colleagues serving as bishops outside the South. He was not outspoken on the events taking place in Alabama during 1964 and 1965 and, like Harmon and other Alabama church leaders, was not receptive to clergy of his own denomination coming to the state from other venues to participate in civil rights demonstrations. But he worked quietly behind the scenes to persuade segregationists like George Wallace to forestall violence against the demonstrators and discouraged his Methodist flock from supporting attempts by local authorities to use force to further racial injustice.

The other talent that Goodson displayed was a political astuteness as to what would be needed within his own church to accomplish the unity of white and black membership. To a certain point in the process, Goodson was willing to adopt a gradualist approach, initiating joint conversations with leaders of the Central Alabama Conference, the integration of Christian education training programs at Camp Sumatanga, and amiable meetings with well-known segregationists in his conferences. Meanwhile, he prepared the way for a resolution of the official mandate from General Conference by reshaping his district superintendents and advisory staff with a much younger and enlightened group of ministers and laity. While he was willing to draw support from such older and more experienced progressives as John Rutland, Denson Franklin, and Harry Denman, in 1967 and 1968 the bishop moved rapidly to fill his cabinet with district superintendents from a newer generation of dynamic leaders who considered it part of the mission of their ministries to integrate the conferences as quickly as possible. The presence of these younger men in his inner circle had an unexpected consequence for Goodson: they often pushed him to move more rapidly on merger than he was prepared to do; and there were sometimes meetings, like the one in 1970 in Florence, where the bishop had to face their sharp criticism. For an expansive ego, Goodson no doubt found these moments uncomfortable, but he seemed to have decided that the merger process would never succeed if he did not have the more dynamic younger generation on his side.

Goodson realized that his two white conferences would have to be informed about the necessity of merger within the context of Christian teachings. The bishop's 1968 and 1969 convocations on racial reconciliation brought many black and white Methodists together for the first time in a social setting to talk about the equality of all human beings within the universal church. In the end, Goodson announced his own personal commitment to racial integration and merger in statements he made during his episcopacy, starting with the pastoral letter in 1965 after the Selma confrontation. Selma was a transforming event for Goodson. His columns and letters from that point on to the final North Alabama Conference vote for merger in 1971 focused on a constant theme: the centrality of race as the social issue of his time and the necessity for the "community of the faithful" to lead in achieving racial justice. Goodson realized fully the impact of the civil rights movement in the South on society and church. His willingness to take a public stand against the violence unleashed against civil rights workers in Selma and elsewhere aligned the bishop solidly in support of the movement. At a deeper level, Goodson's inner core of decency and justice was shaken by his encounters with the diehard segregationists in his denomination. Yet the close NAC merger vote did not seem to cause Goodson any doubts that he had chosen the right path to lead the church in a direction that challenged the ethos of the old Southern social order.

THE IRONY IS THAT winning the merger fight did not have the profound consequences for the denomination that Goodson and his supporters—nor his opponents for that matter—had expected. In 1976, the Emory University Center for Research published a report by Grant S. Schockley and Earl Brewer that analyzed the impact of merger on United Methodism. The conclusions were predictable: few churches nationwide had integrated and the positive results had only reached the level of tokenism. The authors observed some progress in impersonal and contractual relationships of church agencies, but little in local churches where relations are "more personal, communal, and voluntary."[28] The report also revealed that nearly half of all black pastors were at least fifty-five years old and that young African Americans were not entering seminaries for lack of financial assistance and because of decreasing opportunities for black ministers as a result of merger. Black district superintendents stated frankly that white Methodists would not accept having a black clergyman baptize their children, perform marriage ceremonies, or preside at funerals. The year following, the *Birmingham News* published an article indicating that nothing had really changed in Alabama in the five years since merger. Young black Alabamians were unwilling to go through seven years of college and seminary only to accept a career of serving "small, low-paying black churches."[29] When questioned by the *News*, the Reverend Bill Davis, then chair of the Council on Ministries, could name only Birmingham's Norwood United Methodist Church as fully integrated, and he noted the somewhat sporadic attendance of black college students in Tuscaloosa at the predominantly white Trinity United Methodist.

At century's end, the church had changed, but not as rapidly as Goodson and his supporters would have wanted. The unwillingness of the conference leadership to give black ministers an opportunity to occupy significant positions led by the 1990s to an exodus of promising young black preachers from Alabama. Many were convinced that much had been lost in the decades after the end of the CAC. In an interview in the *Birmingham News*, Chester E. Brown, pastor of St. Paul, admitted that "we lost everything—we lost the positions and the prestige."[30] Eighteen years after merger, the *News* noted in a retrospective article by religion editor Greg Garrison that no black United Methodist bishops had been assigned to Alabama, only two blacks had been appointed as district superintendents, and there had been no cross-racial ministerial appointments. The Reverend Charles Lee was only the second district superintendent appointed in 1989, a full decade after Moses C. Barrett stepped down in 1979. Charles Hutchinson, who had at one time been the outstanding candidate for a district superintendent appointment, decided to leave the state for Indiana, where the conference had far fewer blacks than in north Alabama. That assessment did change two years later, in 1992, when William Wesley Morris was appointed bishop of the Alabama-West Florida Conference, the first African American. South Alabama had been the most reluctant of the three conferences to approve merger, but ironically it had become one of the few in the Southeastern Jurisdiction to have a resident black bishop.

By 1990, only about 6,000 blacks were members of the North Alabama Conference—about 3.5 percent of its 168,000 congregants. As African American Bishop Joseph Bethea of South Carolina pointed out to the *News,* black ministers were still mostly assigned to all-black churches that were not large or influential. The harshest criticism of the conference came from one of the nation's most influential African American leaders, a person who had been vital to the merger battle of the 1960s, namely former St. Paul Methodist pastor Joseph Lowery, who had since left the state for a church in Atlanta and to head the SCLC. He thought that merger had been driven in the Deep South by an inclination toward "tokenism." This tendency "to keep just one black leader at a time" had the effect, Lowery maintained, of "stripping blacks of leadership at key levels" and placing the election of black leadership in white hands." The problem was, from Lowery's point of view, a serious one: the church was insensitive and weak in fulfilling its official policies of "racial inclusiveness."[31] He deplored that Methodists had lost the momentum of the Goodson years and believed that the denomination was regressing. Thus for Lowery and too many others, the end of the black conferences proved to be a token, Pyrrhic victory.

THE OUTCOME OF THE long struggle to unite Alabama Methodists racially has to be judged a qualified success. To the most enthusiastic of the white supporters of merger, the most important objective had been obtained: Methodist churches were open to people of all races without exception. More than that, before Bishop Goodson departed, virtually all the Methodist institutions in the state were integrated: colleges, retirement homes, the children's home, and camps.[32] For black ministers of the CAC, merger meant increased (though not equivalent) salaries, participation in an adequately funded retirement system, and even conference financial support for formal education.

But as the Reverend Ted Leach commented, merger was a "non-event as far as the day-to-day life of most Methodist churches."[33] There were difficulties in achieving a true union of the races that went beyond what Goodson and the tri-conference committee could accomplish in even the best of organizational plans. Merger came for whites and blacks with a longtime legacy of distrust between the races in the church. The black ministers and laity of the Central Alabama Conference had been apprehensive about entering a white-controlled organization in which they were vastly outnumbered. Chester Brown recalled that many blacks were fearful that the white conferences would "take away from us all we got." There were sensitive memories within the black community of condescension and a "missionary attitude" from whites toward the former CAC churches. After merger, Brown remembered that Claude Whitehead called him and offered to bring a group of his white parishioners over to Brown's church in Alexander City for a worship service. Brown was agreeable, but members of his church insisted that they go to Whitehead's church for the service. The sentiment in the black church was that they "were tired of them going to us; let us go to them." African Americans also sensed that whites were very "tense and concerned about merger—more so than blacks." There was a need for whites to "constantly sell and re-sell merger" to their congregations.[34]

One area not often discussed in the *Advocate* articles was the difference in the style of worship found in black and white churches. This was a point of view that was frequently expressed in the white community before and after merger: blacks would not be happy in a white church setting that was more formal and liturgical than were the black church services. As George Russell had rationalized in 1972, each race had its own "lifestyle and way of doing things." So each black church had its own lifestyle rooted in tradition and the black experience.[35] Bishop Goodson did not accept these differences as an impediment to racial union. He was open to all styles of worship and had particularly enjoyed the meetings of the Central Conference when he was their bishop.

Although Kenneth Goodson could not and would not have claimed credit personally for the success of the merger vote in 1972, Methodists would have not moved toward merger as expeditiously and openly as they did in the years from 1964 to 1972 without his leadership. One of his protégées, Bob Morgan, remembered going to a football game in Tuscaloosa after the passage of merger. Goodson (who liked to arrive early and stay until the grounds crew cleaned up the stands afterward) noticed that perhaps a third of the spectators were black. The bishop turned to Morgan and asked him, "Bob, look around—what was the problem?"[36] By the time of his death in 1991, many Methodists in Alabama remembered Goodson most for his courageous stands on behalf of full integration of the church. As a Tuscaloosa newspaper proclaimed in its report of Goodson's passing, "Those who knew and respected him will always thank God for sending him to Alabama."[37] Sometimes one person can make a big difference.

## NOTES

1.   Morgan interview tape, May 9, 2001, Robinson , NACA.

2.   Ibid.

3.   Davis interview tape, May 9, 2001, Robinson , NACA.

4.   Hunter interview tape, April 25, 2001, Robinson , NACA.

5.   Reeves interview tape, May 7, 2001, Robinson , NACA.

6.   Elmore interview tape, April 6, 2001, Robinson , NACA.

7.   *Alabama Christian Advocate*, January 15, 1974.

8.   Eva Walker interview tape, May 23, 2001, Robinson, NACA.

9.   Betty Copeland interview, Nicholas, February 27, 1996, NACA.

10.  Wayne Flynt. *Alabama Baptists: Southern Baptists in the Heart of Dixie* (Tuscaloosa: University of Alabama Press, 1998) 459, 464.

11.  Mark Newman. *Getting Right with God; Southern Baptists and Desegregation, 1945–1995* (Tuscaloosa: University of Alabama Press, 2001), 168.

12.  Flynt, *Alabama Baptists*, 538. Flynt writes, "Having never been the object of racism themselves and knowing little about how blacks were constantly subjected to it, they took for granted what was deeply offensive to African Americans. Passive racism simply accepted the inferiority of African Americans as a people whether the cause was genetic or lack of cultural and educational opportunities (518–519).

13.  Ibid., 468.

14.  Ibid., 470.

15.  This in fact occurred in 1970 in one of the most publicized conflicts over church membership in the denomination involving Birmingham First Baptist Church. The dispute involved the issue of membership for an African American woman and her daughter who had been attending services there, and the result was a debate within the

congregation and the defeat of a resolution to accept members without reference to race by a narrow vote of 249 against to 217 in favor. The bitter outcome was the exodus of some 250 members from First Baptist to form a completely biracial church, the Baptist Church of the Covenant in downtown Birmingham (Flynt, *Alabama Baptists*, 519).

16. Joel Alvis Jr. *Religion and Race: Southern Presbyterians, 1946–1983* (Tuscaloosa: University of Alabama, 1994), 50, 6.

17. Ibid., 73. 93.

18. Bass, *Blessed Are the Peacemakers*, 85–86, 210–211.

19. Alvis, *Religion and Race,* 132–133. As Alvis points out, race was not the only issue that was involved in the separation, but the debate over race precipitated the split.

20. Gardiner H. Shattuck Jr., *Episcopalians and Race: Civil War to Civil Rights* (Lexington: University Press of Kentucky, 2000), 13, 31.

21. Gardener H. Shattuck Jr., "Serving God in the Word: Theology and Civil Rights Activism in the Episcopal Church, 1958–1973," *Anglican and Episcopal History*, 64, no. 3 (1995): 331, 333.

22. Shattuck, *Episcopalians and Race,* 154.

23. The experience of Alabama Episcopalians during the civil rights era, and especially the role of Bishop Carpenter, is expertly handled by J. Barry Vaughn in his *Bishops, Bourbons, and Big Mules: A History of the Episcopal Church in Alabama* (Tuscaloosa: University of Alabama Press, 2013), 133–167.

24. Shattuck, *Episcopalians and Race,* 154; Bass, *Blessed Are the Peacemakers*, 30, 32.

25. Vaughan, *Bishops, Bourbons, and Big Mules*, 156–164.

26. Quoted in Bass, *Blessed Are the Peacemakers,* 211.

27. Newman, *Getting Right with God,* 67.

28. Grant S. Schockley and Earl D. C. Brewer, *Study of Black Pastors and Churches in the Methodist Church* (Atlanta: Center for Research at Emory University, 1976), 7.

29. *Birmingham News,* July 7, 1977.

30. Ibid., October 14, 1990.

31. Ibid.

32. Elmore interview tape, April 6, 2001, Robinson. NACA; Mitchell, "We Are at Our Best," 34.

33. Ted Leach interview tape, April 25, 2001, Robinson. NACA.

34. Chester Brown interview tape, Robinson, April 23, 2001, NACA.

35. *Alabama Christian Advocate*, January 15, 1974.

36. Morgan interview tape, May 9, 2001, Robinson, NACA,

37. Tuscaloosa News, September 18, 1991.

# Works Consulted

## MANUSCRIPT SOURCES

North Alabama Conference Archives, Birmingham-Southern College, Birmingham, Alabama

Bishops Papers and Correspondence

Goodson, W. Kenneth. Papers.

Hodge, Bachman G., Papers.

Brannon, Leo. "Study Document Prepared for the Tri-Conference Advisory Committee on Merger," March 18, 1969. Typescript.

Elmore, Joe. "Crossings: A Personal Journey Toward Grace." Undated manuscript.

Montgomery, Ed, Papers.

"Summary of the Relation of the Central Alabama Conference to the Alabama-West Florida Conference," n.d.

Lynn-Hendley Research Library. Birmingham Public Library, Birmingham, Alabama.

Southern Regional Council Papers.

Whitehead, Claude. "Memories of Alexander City First Methodist Church, 1962–1967," Undated manuscript in possession of author.


## INTERVIEWS WITH METHODIST MINISTERS AND LAITY

*There are two sources for the interviews cited: personal interviews by the author and tapes of interviews by J. Mitchell Robinson. Both are housed in the North Alabama Conference Archives, Birmingham-Southern College, Birmingham, Alabama.*

Branscomb, Louise. Interview by Nicholas, March 19, 1996.

Brown, Chester. Tape of interview, Robinson, April 23, 2001.

Copeland, Betty. Interview by Nicholas, February 17, 1996.

Davis, Bill. Tape of interview, Robinson, April 9, 2001.

Elmore, Joe. Tape of Interview, Robinson, April 6, 2001.

———. Interviews by Nicholas, March 1, 1996 and May 8, 2002.

Franklin, Denson. Interview by Nicholas, April 30, 1996.

Goodwin, Burt. Interview by Nicholas, April 13, 2002.

Goodwin, Ray. Interview by Nicholas, September 21, 2002.

Hunter, Duncan. Tape of interview, Robinson, April 25, 2001.

———. Interview by Nicholas, October 25, 1996.

Leech, Ted. Tape of interview, Robinson, April 15, 2001.

Montgomery, Ed. Tape of interview, Robinson, April 11, 2001.

_____. Interview by Nicholas, February 18, 2002.

Morgan, Bob. Tape of interview, Robinson, May 9, 2001.

Rutland, John. Interview by Nicholas, February 22, 1996.

Reeves, Nina. Tape of interview, Robinson, April 15, 2001.

Vann, David. Tape of Interview given by Ruth Vann Lillian to Robinson.

Walker, Eva. Tape of Interview, Robinson, May 23, 2001.

Whitehead, Claude. Interview by Nicholas, June 2, 2003.

## Primary Publications

*Alabama Christian Advocate*, 1950–1974.

*Birmingham News*, 1954–1974.

*Daily Proceedings of the Annual Sessions of the Central Alabama Conference of the United Methodist Church.* 1950–1974.

High, Stanley. "Methodism's Pink Fringe," *Readers Digest* 56 (February 1950): 134–138.

*Journals of the North Alabama Conference of the Methodist Church*, 1939–1974.

King, Martin Luther, Jr. *Why We Can't Wait.* New York: Penguin Books, 1964.

Methodist Layman's Union. *A Pronouncement.* Birmingham, Alabama, Methodist Layman's Union, 1959.

Prestwood, Charles Marion, Jr. "Social Ideas of Methodist Ministers in Alabama since Unification," Ph.D. dissertation, Boston University, 1960.

Salisbury, Harrison. "Fear and Hatred Grip Birmingham." *New York Times*, April 12, 1960.

## Secondary Publications

Alvis, Joel L., Jr. *Religion and Race: Southern Presbyterians, 1946–1983.* Tuscaloosa: University of Alabama Press, 1994.

Arsenault, Raymond. *Freedom Riders: 1961 and the Struggle for Racial Justice.* New York: Oxford University Press, 2006.

Bass, Jonathan S. "Bishop C. C. J. Carpenter: From Segregation to Integration." *Alabama Review* 45 (July 1992): 184–215.

_____. *Blessed are the Peacemakers: Martin Luther King, Eight White Religious Leaders and the "Letter from the Birmingham Jail."* Baton Rouge: Louisiana State University Press, 2001.

Bauman, Mark K. *Warren Akin Candler: The Conservative as Idealist.* Metuchen, NJ: Scarecrow Press, 1981.

_____ and Berkeley Kalin (eds.). *Quiet Voices: Southern Rabbis and Black Civil Rights, 1880s to 1960s, Judaic Studies Series.* Tuscaloosa: University of Alabama Press, 1997.

Blackwelder, Julia Kirk. "Southern White Fundamentalists and the Civil Rights Movement," *Phylon* 40, no. 4 (December 1979): 334–341.

Branch, Taylor. *Parting the Waters: America in the King Years, 1954–1963.* New York: Simon and Schuster, 1988.

Chappel, David L. *Inside Agitators: White Southerners in the Civil Rights Movement.* Baltimore: Johns Hopkins University Press, 1994.

Clark, Elmer T. *A Methodist Romance: A History of Paine College.* Augusta, Georgia: Paine College, 1932.

Collins, Donald. *When the Church Bell Rang Racist: The Methodist Church and Civil Rights in Alabama.* Macon, Georgia: Mercer University Press, 2005.

Eagles, Charles W. *Outside Agitator: Jon Daniels and the Civil Rights Movement in Alabama.* Chapel Hill: University of North Carolina Press, 1993.

Ellis, Carol. "The Tragedy of the White Moderate: Father Albert Foley and Martin Luther King, Birmingham, 1963." *Gulf South Historical Review* 19 (Fall 2003): 7–30.

Ellwanger, Walter H. "Lutheranism in Alabama and Other Parts of the South," *Concordia Historical Institute Quarterly* 48, no. 2 (Summer 1975): 35–43.

Eskew, Glenn T. *But for Birmingham: The Local and National Movements in the Civil Rights Struggle.* Chapel Hill: University of North Carolina Press, 1997.

Fallin, Wilson, Jr. *The African-American Church in Birmingham, Alabama, 1815–1963: A Shelter in the Storm.* New York, Garland, 1997.

Flynt, Wayne. *Alabama Baptists: Southern Baptists in the Heart of Dixie.* Tuscaloosa: University of Alabama Press, 1998.

Garrow, David J. *Bearing the Cross: Martin Luther King, Jr., and the Southern Christian Leadership Conference.* New York: W. Morrow, 1986.

Goldfield, David. *Black, White and Southern: Race Relations and Southern Culture, 1940 to the Present.* Baton Rouge: Louisiana State University Press, 1990.

Harmon, Nolan B. *Ninety Years and Counting.* Nashville: Upper Room, 1983.

Hemphill, Paul. *Leaving Birmingham: Notes of a Native Son.* New York: Viking Press, 1993.

Hill, Samuel. *Southern Churches in Crisis.* New York: Holt, Rinehart and Winston, 1966.

Lakey, Othal Hawthorne, *The History of the CME Church.* Louisville, Kentucky: CME Publishing House, 1985.

Lazenby, Marion Elias. *History of Methodism in Alabama and West Florida.* Birmingham: North Alabama Conference and Alabama-West Florida Conference, 1960.

Lowery, Joseph E. *Singing the Lord's Song in a New Land.* Nashville: Abingdon Press, 2011.

Manis, Andrew Michael. *A Fire You Can't Put Out: the Civil Rights Life of Birmingham's Reverend Fred Shuttlesworth.* Tuscaloosa: University of Alabama Press, 1999.

Marsh, Charles. *God's Long Summer: Stories of Faith and Civil Rights.* Princeton, New Jersey: Princeton University Press, 1997.

McBeth, Leon. "Southern Baptists and Race since 1947." *Baptist History and Heritage* 7 (July 1972): 155–69.

Marshall, James Williams. *The Presbyterian Church in Alabama*. Montgomery: Presbyterian Historical Society of Alabama, 1977.

McWhorter, Diane. *Carry Me Home: Birmingham, Alabama: The Climatic Battle of the Civil Rights Revolution*. New York: Simon & Schuster, 2001.

Moore, Andrew S. *The South's Tolerable Alien: Roman Catholics in Alabama and Georgia, 1945–1970*. Baton Rouge: Louisiana State University Press, 2007.

Morgan, Charles, Jr. *A Time to Speak*. New York: Harper and Row, 1964.

Mitchell, Joseph. *There is an Election: Episcopal Elections in the Southeastern Jurisdiction of the United Methodist Church*. Troy, Alabama: Leader Press, 1980.

Murray, Peter C. *Methodists and the Crucible of Race, 1930–1975*. Columbia: University of Missouri Press, 2004.

_____. "The Racial Crisis in the Methodist Church." *Methodist History* 26 (October 1987): 3–14.

Newman, Mark. *Getting Right with God: Southern Baptists and Desegregation, 1945–1995*. Tuscaloosa: University of Alabama Press, 2001.

Padgett, Charles Stephen. "Hidden from History, Shielded from Harm: Desegregation at Spring Hill College, 1954–1957." *Alabama Review* 56, no. 4 (October 2003): 278–310.

Russell, Patti B. (ed.). *Walter Kenneth Goodson: A Life*. Commemorative Edition of Virginia Conference Historical Society. Richmond: Virginia Conference Historical Society, 1993.

Rutland, John. *Mary and Me: Telling the Story of Prevenient Grace*. Pensacola: Ardara House, 1996.

Schockley, Grant S. and Earl D. C. Brewer. *Study of Black Pastors and Churches in the Methodist Church*. Atlanta: Center for Research at Emory University, 1976.

Shattuck, Gardener H., Jr. *Episcopalians and Race: Civil War to Civil Rights*. Lexington: University Press of Kentucky, 2000.

_____. "Serving God in the World: Theology and Civil Rights Activism in the Episcopal Church, 1958–1973. *Anglican and Episcopal History* 64, no. 3 (1995): 326–351.

Thomas, James S. *Methodism's Racial Dilemma*. Nashville, Tennessee: Abingdon Press, 1992.

Thornton, J. Mills. *Dividing Lines: Municipal Politics and the Struggle for Civil Rights in Birmingham, Montgomery, and Selma*. Tuscaloosa: University of Alabama Press, 2002.

Tuell, Jack M. *The Organization of the United Methodist Church*. Nashville: Abingdon Press, 1982.

Valentine, Foy D. *A Historical Study of Southern Baptists and Race Relations, 1917-1947*. New York: Arno Press, 1980.

Vaughn, J. Barry. *Bishops, Bourbons, and Big Mules: A History of the Episcopal Church in Alabama*. Tuscaloosa: University of Alabama Press, 2013.

*Walter Kenneth Goodson: A Life*. Commemorative Edition, *Virginia United Methodist Heritage*, 1993.

White, Marjorie Longenecker. *Birmingham Revolutionaries: The Reverend Fred Shuttlesworth and the Alabama Movement for Christian Rights*. Macon, Georgia: Mercer University Press, 2000.

Williams, Juan. *Eyes on the Prize: America's Civil Rights Years, 1954–1965*. New York: Penguin Books, 1988.

Wilson, Robert L. *Methodists and Foreign Policy since World War II*. http://www.cmpage.org/biasese/chapter2.html.

Wogaman, J. Philip. *Methodism's Challenge in Race Relations: A Study of Strategy*. Boston: Boston University Press, 1960.

# Index